"An easy-to-connect-with, teen/adult read with which to explore the community from which we've developed, who we are and what we – with the reader – might yet become!" – Rev. Carolyn McBean, retired, Regina, SK

"An informative and funny look at the United Church." – Rev. Shannon McCarthy Executive Secretary, Conference of Manitoba and Northwestern Ontario, Winnipeg, Man.

"For over 90 years this intriguing experiment in how to be church has stood the test of time, and Ralph Milton's book helps us understand how and why." – Rev. Dr. Donald Schmidt, Minister of Worship and Leadership Development, First United Church, Kelowna, BC

"Ralph's book is an excellent resource in understanding where the church has been and where it might be heading. A must read, both from a theological and community perspective, for those who are seeking to understand this United Church of ours." – Rev. Dr. Bill Smith, Executive Secretary of the Bay of Quinte Conference, Belleville, Ont.

"This is Ralph Milton's fourth attempt to describe the church he loves and serves. Each one has been right on. It has taken four books because the United Church is constantly changing, and no one has succeeded as well at capturing a snapshot of a moving target." – Dr. Jim Taylor, author and editor, Lake Country, BC

"A fun and loving family portrait of how our beloved church smiles into the camera at this moment in our life together." – Mardi Tindal, 40th Moderator of the United Church, Columnist for The United Church Observer, Courage and Renewal Facilitator, Toronto, Ont.

"The United Church of Canada isn't about to expire any time soon as long as it continues to speak to the experiences of the people and remembers that the church we call "ours" is in relationship with Creator God in whom we belong and have our home." – Kim Uyede-Kai, Minister for Congregational Support, Hamilton Conference, The United Church of Canada

"Ralph's book captures the ethos of our beloved church; just as Jesus laid down the ethos and orthopraxis for those who wished to follow him in the fourth chapter of Luke verses 18–19." – Rev. Laird Russell-Yearwood served two pastoral charges over 23 years of ministry, and now lives in Brandon, Manitoba.

RALPH MILTON

THIS United Church OF OURS

FOURTH EDITION

WOOD LAKE

Editor: Mike Schwartzentruber
Designer: Robert MacDonald
Proofreader: Dianne Greenslade

Library and Archives Canada Cataloguing in Publication
Milton, Ralph, author
This United Church of ours / Ralph Milton. – Fourth edition.
Includes bibliographical references.
Issued in print and electronic formats.
ISBN 978-1-77064-917-0 (paperback). – ISBN 978-1-77064-918-7 (html)
1. United Church of Canada. I. Title.
BX9881.M54 2016   287.9'2   C2016-906881-1   C2016-906882-X

Published by Wood Lake Publishing Inc.
485 Beaver Lake Road, Kelowna, BC, Canada, V4V 1S5
www.woodlake.com | 250.766.2778

Wood Lake Publishing acknowledges the financial support of the Government of
Canada through the Canada Book Fund (CBF) for its publishing activities. Wood
Lake Publishing acknowledges the financial support of the Province of British
Columbia through the Book Publishing Tax Credit.

At Wood Lake Publishing, we practice what we publish, being guided by a
concern for fairness, justice, and equal opportunity in all of our relationships
with employees and customers. Wood Lake Publishing is committed to caring
for the environment and all creation. Wood Lake Publishing recycles and reuses,
and encourages readers to do the same. Books are printed on 100% post-
consumer recycled paper, whenever possible. A percentage of all profit is
donated to charitable organizations.

Printing 10 9 8 7 6 5 4 3 2 1
Printed in Canada by Friesens

TABLE OF CONTENTS

DEDICATION

With profound thanks to all the saints in the worldwide church,
and especially in the United Church of Canada, who have loved,
nurtured and tolerated me through eight decades of life.

ACKNOWLEDGEMENTS

This fourth edition of *This United Church of Ours* was not a one-person effort. I wrote the basic text, but more than two dozen people from across the church read the manuscript and enriched it with their comments, criticisms, and suggestions. My sincere thanks to all for your wise feedback:

Rev. Daniel Benson, minister, St. Paul's United Church, Scarborough, Ontario
Rev. Ed Bentley, retired clergy, Belleville, Ontario
Rt. Rev. Jordan Cantwell, moderator, The United Church of Canada
Rev. Jeff Cook, minister, Transcona Memorial United Church, Winnipeg, Manitoba
Brenda Curtis, DM, Westminster United Church, Humboldt, Saskatchewan
Rev. Gordon Dunbar, associate minister for pastoral care and outreach, Port Nelson United Church, Burlington, Ontario; and president of Hamilton Conference
Rev. Rosemary Lambie, executive secretary, Synode Montreal & Ottawa Conference, Montreal, Quebec
Rev. Heather Leffler, President Elect of Hamilton Conference, Rockwood and Stone United, Rockwood, Ontario
Rev. Elizabeth Macdonald, retired, Eastern Ontario
Barbara MacNaughton, DLM-R, spiritual director, minister, St. Andrew's United Church, Easton, Saskatchewan
Rev. Lynn Maki, former executive secretary, Alberta and Northwest Conference, Edmonton, Alberta
Rev. David Martyn, retired clergy, Kelowna, British Columbia
Rev. Carolyn McBean, retired, Regina, Saskatchewan
Rev. Shannon McCarthy, executive secretary, Conference of Manitoba and Northwestern Ontario, Winnipeg, Manitoba
Rev. Beverley Milton, minister emeritus, First United Church, Kelowna, British Columbia
Dr. Brad Morrison, Grace United Church, Sarnia, Ontario; assistant professor of practical theology, Huron University College, Western University, London, Ontario
Rev. Pegi Ridout, interim minister throughout Hamilton Conference; faculty, Interim Ministry Network; associate with L3 Consulting Group
Dee Robertson, retired educator, Humboldt, Saskatchewan
Rev. Dr. Donald Schmidt, minister of worship and leadership development, First United Church, Kelowna, British Columbia

Rev. Dr. Bill Smith, executive secretary, Bay of Quinte Conference, Belleville, Ontario
Rev. Cheryl-Ann Stadelbauer Sampa, executive secretary, London Conference, London, Ontario
Dr. Jim Taylor, author and editor, Lake Country, British Columbia
Mardi Tindal, former moderator of the United Church; columnist for *The United Church Observer*; Courage and Renewal Facilitator, Toronto, Ontario
Kim Uyede-Kai, minister for congregational support, Hamilton Conference
Rev. Laird Russell-Yearwood, retired, Brandon, Manitoba

FOREWORD

Ralph Milton once said to me, "You and I, among others, have never fit the various slots in the United Church nomenclature, because we are often working for the church, directly or indirectly, and we are lay people, not in the sense of being uninformed about the work in question, but technically in that we have not been 'done.'"

Ralph hasn't been "done" (ordained) and I'm glad he isn't done with our church, either. While he doesn't fit easily into any of our church's role-titles, there's no one who better understands and loves the soul of our church, or who can describe it more clearly. And his deep understanding is always served with a generous helping of irresistible humour. If I were in charge of handing out fictional United Church titles, I'd anoint Ralph "The Most Irreverent" and trust he'd be delighted.

This new edition of the beloved *This United Church of Ours* is just what we need. If ever there was a time for us to laugh and to remember who we are, this is it. Humour and humility are married in these pages, reflecting the original sense of humour (bodily fluid) and humility (being "grounded," from the word humus, of earth). Our body of faith is both grounded and fluid; our ways of doing things spring from deep roots and adapt to changing contexts; at our best, we are both serious and lighthearted.

You will read here about who we are as an increasingly diverse community of faith within a changing national landscape.

The congregation in which I worship welcomes new members frequently, and we should give every one of them a copy of this book. For newcomers, it offers a better understanding of our idiosyncrasies and core beliefs, from worship to money to ethical concerns. For long-timers, it reminds us about why we do what we do. Ralph does all of this with honesty, creativity, and personal revelation of his own love and frustrations.

Whenever I feel confused or alone, one of the things I do is pull out family albums or flip open my phone to see more recent photos. I long for the faces of those I love and enjoy, to remember how my story is linked to theirs, and what our story together means. Reading this book is like that. It reminds me who I'm connected to, through the love of Christ, in a great, evolving story of which we are each a part. It has me smiling and laughing out loud. It makes me sad and reflective sometimes, too, reminding me of the words in our *Song of Faith*, that we are "a community of broken but hopeful believers."

Finally it makes me weep over the beauty of it all and why I love this church. May you fall in love, too, and be blessed.

Mardi Tindal
Former Moderator of the United Church of Canada
(2009–2012)

1

Nuts and Bolts

For just as the body is one and has many members,
and all the members of the body, though many, are one body,
so it is with Christ.
For in the one Spirit we were all baptized into one body…
1 Corinthians 12:12–13

I was a "greeter" at the church door that Sunday morning. Up the steps came a couple, each holding a Starbucks coffee mug. "Is it okay to bring these into church?" they asked.

"Hey, why not?" I said. "Maybe we should set up a Starbucks concession right here the lobby."

"Cool!" he said.

"My mother would have a fit," she said.

"Your mother isn't here," I said. "Anyway, lots of things she told you about the church probably aren't true anymore."

"Like what?" she asked.

"Hang around," I said. "You'll find out."

After church over coffee (not Starbucks, this time, but good coffee nonetheless) I found out their names: Janice and Colin.

"You were sure right about things being different," said Colin. "The music was upbeat. It was way more informal. I mean, who would've thought you could wear ratty jeans and a T-shirt to church."

"Yeah, but, it still felt like home," added Janice. "People were friendly, and the service had all the parts I remember from when I was a kid. But like you said, it sure was different. I liked it. I think we'll come back."

"I hope you do," I said.

The same but different

It's a dance.

It's a dance the United Church of Canada has been doing since it got started way back in 1925. Trying to keep the best of the old while being open to new ideas, new thoughts, new music, new ways to worship, and new ways to live the life of faith.

We don't always get it right. Sometimes we hang on to ideas and traditions way past their "best before" date. Sometimes we run way ahead of the pack and do things or say things that seem to come from way out in left field.

We are what we are. It's a faith community I love and that has nurtured me for many years. It's not perfect, just like my own family isn't perfect. I love my family; I love my church, because with them, I am "home."

A personal statement

Throughout this book, I'll tell you about my own church community, which happens to be First United Church in the city of

Kelowna, British Columbia. Not because it's better or worse than any other church, but only because it's where I live.

It's my job to describe this United Church of ours as candidly as I can. I'm a well-seasoned journalist – a professional writer with a well-tuned BS detector – so I'll not intentionally do a snow job on you.

But I'm also human, and this is my tribe I'm writing about, made up of folk I love in an institution (I like to call it an organism) that has nurtured me for many years. I won't try to hide that, but I'll try to be honest.

A whole bunch of United Church folk from across the country had a look at this book before it went to press (see Acknowledgements). I paid close attention to their comments, because I wanted *This United Church of Ours* (the fourth edition!) to give a fair picture of what our church is really like. But this book has no official status. It has not been approved by any church body and it's been produced by an independent publisher.

In the end, this is my own personal statement. I've not tried to hide my own opinions and viewpoints. They are my own, so please don't blame them on anybody else. Please take them all with the proverbial grain of salt.

There are exceptions to just about everything I say in this book. It's entirely possible you may run across a United Church congregation or United Church people that are not like anything you read about in this book. We're a very diverse church. And there's far more that could be said about every one of the topics I deal with. What you have here is a very brief, once-over-lightly picture of a multi-textured, many flavoured organism.

What do I wear?

This first chapter is here because my long-time friend and colleague, Jim Taylor, read over the first draft and said, "You're not answering the questions people ask! People want practical stuff. Like, what do you wear?"

I'd never given that much thought, to tell you the truth. I stumble into the closet Sunday morning and take the first thing that comes into my hand, put it on, stumble out of the closet, and Bev (my spouse) says, "You can't wear that!"

So I stumble back in, grab something else, and repeat the process until Bev either gives up or I find myself wearing something she considers suitable. But because of Jim's question, I went to church last Sunday and actually looked at what people had on.

I'm no wiser. I saw everything from blue jeans and sloppy sweatshirts to three-piece suits to hats and white gloves, to...well you name it. (Actually, it was the people in the bell choir who had the white gloves.) One of our teenage regulars has hardware in her nose and ears, and her hair dyed a different colour every Sunday.

I was told that in a neighbouring church on a hot summer morning the chair of the board went to the pulpit to make an announcement. He was barefoot, with ragged cut-offs and a T-shirt with holes in it. Some laughed. Nobody complained.

So after that "scientific" survey, I can report with confidence that you can wear anything you feel comfortable wearing. There's no such thing as a dress code in the United Church for anyone. Including clergy.

At least, that's the way it is in my own church community. I'm told there are churches where the men wear suits and the women wear nice dresses.

What if you came bare naked?

Well, that would raise some eyebrows, for sure.

A rainbow church

We're a very diverse denomination. That's an important thing to emphasize about the United Church. There are no entry qualifications. None. Everyone is welcome. Everyone!

Some would tell you that means the United Church is wishy-washy with no standards. There may be some truth in that.

We are a welcoming church. Others might tell you that's not always the case everywhere. They'll tell you about times they have felt very unwelcome. Unfortunately, that's also true.

But to be welcoming is certainly a goal. I like to think it's because we are a "rainbow church" that celebrates all the wonderful variety in God's creation. We have been wonderfully enriched by the delightful diversity of women and men, some of them "refugees" from more conservative denominations or other communities of faith where they didn't quite fit. That includes a healthy sampling of folks from the LGBTQ community. (LGBTQ stands for Lesbian, Gay, Bisexual, Transgendered, Queer/Questioning.)

If you decide you want to become a full member of the church, you might be asked to take a membership class, and you'd be asked some questions about your faith and your commitment. But this membership is open to everyone.

Where do we sit?

Some months ago, Bev and I visited the historic Ryerson United Church in Vancouver. "This was my grandmother's pew," said Bev as she sat in one of the old oak pews near the middle of the church.

Bev's grandmother has been gone for many years, and so has that tradition of people who "owned" certain pews. But, of course, people are creatures of habit and tend to sit in the same chair or pew every time they come.

But you can sit anywhere you like.

Stand? Sit? Kneel?

First, we don't kneel in the United Church. Well, no, that's not entirely true. For some special events such as confirmation or ordination, the ones being confirmed or ordained may kneel. But not those of us in the pews.

We usually stand up to sing, if for no other reason than that we sing better standing up, and our backsides get tired from sitting too long. Bev has trouble getting up and down, so she makes sure she has a soft cushion under her bum, and then sits through the whole service. When I'm in a strange church and I don't know what the customs are, I just do whatever the others do.

But there's no rule. A friend of mine had a bad back for a while, and he couldn't sit or stand for very long. So he brought along a good fat cushion for his head, and lay down on the front pew.

Whatever works.

Who's who

The bulletin? You could call it a program. It's a pamphlet that tells you who's who, what things are happening in the church, and how the worship service will proceed. It will tell you the names of the hymns and where to find them in the hymn book.

There will be some prayers in which you join. If you're not sure what part to say out loud, just listen, or mumble till you know what's going on. Don't worry about when to stand and sit. Just do what the other folks do.

But even that bulletin is changing. More and more churches are using projectors and computers. In our church, there are two large video screens in the front and one at the back, and everything you need to know – the songs, the prayers, the announcements – *everything* appears on those screens.

We still hand out a bulletin, but its main function is to keep you informed about all the things that happen in the church during the week. And the bulletin will probably give you the church phone number and office hours.

There are many things I can't tell you in this book because each church is different. For instance, the starting times of Sunday services vary from one congregation to the next.

The traditional starting time was 11:00 on Sunday morning, but now many churches worship at 10:00 or 10:30. One church in our area starts at 9:50. Check out the congregational website, or e-mail or phone the church and ask.

You can call anytime because most churches have voice mail that tells you when the service begins. If you have questions about child care during the service, or Sunday school, or parking, call during office hours, which, in smaller churches, may only be weekday mornings. Some churches, though, have no office hours at all.

Communion

If communion is being served, you are invited to participate. Everybody is invited. No exceptions. You don't have to be good or holy or a member. Communion is God's gift of love to you. There are no preconditions.

Even if you aren't sure you are a Christian, the gift is there for you. How you choose to receive this gift, how you decide to participate, whether you take only bread or only juice or both or neither – this is your decision. And you don't have to explain that to anyone.

Service length

As with almost everything else about the United Church, there's tremendous variety in the length of the service from one con-

gregation to another. The so-called "norm" is an hour, but I've been to services that lasted 45 minutes and those that lasted two hours. The length can vary even in the same congregation depending on what's going on that morning.

Can you leave early? Sure. But it's nice to stay through the whole thing and join the folks for coffee afterwards. The coffee time is, for me, one of the best parts of church. That's where we make the connections and build the trust so that we can offer friendship and caring to each other. This "mutual ministry" is far more important than most people realize.

What do you call "the Rev"?

What do you call the minister? Well, for years I called her "Honey," but I wouldn't recommend that unless you happen to be married to her, as I was. Most of the folks in the congregations she served simply called her "Bev," and a few "Rev. Bev." Some parents insisted that their children call her "Mrs. Milton."

Bev is now retired and, like me, a member of the congregation. We call our minister Donald. A few people address him as Rev. Schmidt, although if you want to be picky about it, that isn't correct. The proper form of address when you are speaking to clergy is Dr. Schmidt, or Mrs. Milton, or Mr. Jones, or Ms. Johnson. That's if you want to be formal.

If you are writing or talking about your minister, and you want to be really formal, it would be The Reverend Dr. Schmidt, or The Reverend Beverley Milton. Or something like that. But that kind of formality went out the window years ago.

With people moving over from more evangelical denominations, some folks are using the term "Pastor." That's just fine. I personally like that better than "Reverend."

Singing

Okay, so we've got you dressed, into church on time to get a choice pew halfway between the front and the back, and you know what to call the minister, besides, "Hey, Rev!"

Do you know what a hymn is? No, that is not pronounced "hy-man." That's something very different. It's pronounced "him" and is simply a song we sing in church. The words are often in the form of a prayer addressed to God, but not necessarily. The old hymns are sometimes a bit slow and draggy, but they have nice harmonies. (I like to sing bass.) The newer ones often have more zip.

In the United Church, the most common source of songs is a red book you'll probably find in the pews. It's called *Voices United*, and I think it is a really fine collection of the best of the old and the new. In the bulletin or on the screen, if it says "VU 223" or something like that, the VU refers to *Voices United*.

You might also find a very fine supplement called *More Voices*, which has a glorious collection of new music – foot-stompin' upbeat music, meditative chants, and interesting songs from all over the world.

Worship leaders are free to choose music from wherever they find it, to say nothing of various instruments and those who play them with assorted levels of competence. There's nobody in an office somewhere who says, "You must sing these songs," or "You have to do your music this way!" It's up to the local congregation.

A new resource for small congregations is *Sing Hallelujah*, a video songbook where you see the song-leader on the screen, you hear the music, and the words go trucking across the bottom. It features some of the finest musicians in the church – Linnea Good, Ron Klusmeier, Jim & Jean Strathdee, Bruce Harding, various choirs, and others. All of these musicians have

active websites, so if you want more information just search by their name.

Our francophone congregations and those choosing to sing some hymns in French, mainly (but not exclusively) in Quebec, use *Nos Voix Unis*, which uses many of the same tunes as you'll find in the anglophone hymn books.

The important thing is to enjoy the singing, and to listen to the power of the poetry in the words. It's been said that if you want to know what people believe, listen to the songs they sing. I'd say that's pretty well true of the people in the United Church.

Prayers

When my grandkids were small and they'd say their prayer (usually called "grace") before a meal, they'd sometimes proudly announce, "I closed my eyes." And they'd get a bit of parental affirmation for that.

The custom of closing your eyes when you pray simply comes from the reality that we can concentrate more easily when we do that. It's about mindfulness. But there's no rule.

In fact, you'll notice that in the bulletin or on the screens there are some prayers that you say along with the worship leader. You can't read with your eyes closed.

I like to close my eyes when praying, but I do it simply to keep my mind on the prayer. For me, that's quite a job. My mind tends to wander very easily.

Some people wonder about the prayers that are spoken from the pulpit. Are they simply putting words into our mouths? Don't we communicate directly with God?

Excellent questions. For me, the prayers from the pulpit stimulate reflections in my own head about my own life, and I find plenty of concerns to express. The prayers I hear prompt my personal prayers, and often put words around what I feel.

The sermon

Speaking of wandering minds, my mind often wanders during
the sermon. That doesn't mean the sermon is dull. It simply
means that something the minister says gets me thinking about
things in my own life, and so I stay with that thought for a bit
before I rejoin the sermon already in progress!

A sermon is something more than a speech or a lecture. It's
not the minister pouring information or ideas into your head
out of some kind of a jug. It's certainly not some authority laying down the law.

I bring my struggles, my life, my fears and hopes into the
church. All of that connects with the images and ideas in the
prayers, hymns, and sermon. And in that mixture, very often
the Spirit of God speaks to me.

In other words, sometimes the best sermons are the ones
that happen in your head, when your life and experience meets
the minister's life and experience, and you let God make the
connections. You'd be surprised what God can communicate,
when you let that happen!

And no, you don't have to believe everything the preacher
says. Ministers are human, and they get confused, just like the
rest of us.

The lectionary

You may notice, as you continue going to church, that there are
Bible readings every Sunday – sometimes three or four of them,
but increasingly just one or two. You may hear them referred to
as the "lectionary readings."

A lectionary is a set of readings from the Bible suggested for
each Sunday, so that in the course of three years, you'll have
heard many, if not most, of the important parts of the Bible.
Most of the major Protestant denominations follow the *Revised*

Common Lectionary, which was put together by a committee representing most of the major Christian churches.

In some denominations, those lectionary readings are a requirement, but in the United Church they are an optional guideline.

Many congregations have Bible study groups, which give people an opportunity to discuss together the readings coming up the next Sunday. I enjoy those discussions very much because they make the whole service more meaningful.

The collection

Then there's the sticky question, "How much do I have to put on the plate when they pass it around?"

The answer is easy. Nothing. Most congregations struggle really hard to pay the bills, and they need all the help they can get. But there's no admission charge. So some people just pass the plate along because they're broke. Nobody expects them to contribute. We're glad they're there, whether they put anything on the plate or not.

Bev and I simply pass the plate along when it comes. Instead of putting something on the plate, we give the church a set of postdated cheques every few months. Others arrange to have automatic deductions made from their chequing accounts. Those deductions are called PAR: Pre-Authorized Remittance. In fact, the people who don't put anything on the plate probably contribute more to the church than those who do.

In some congregations, they don't pass the plate at all. Instead, they may provide a box, suitably labelled, into which people can put their contribution.

So when you are tentatively feeling your way into the church, don't let the offering plate or that offering box spook you. Anything you can contribute will be appreciated, but if you are

broke, you won't be the only one who doesn't put anything in the pot. (If you'd like a tax receipt, there are usually envelopes in the pew that'll help make that happen.)

And read Chapter 9 on money, because there's a bunch of important stuff to be said about this.

By the way, we never call it the "collection" in the United Church. It's called the "offering." (Sorry. That's pretty nit-picky. Call it anything you want.)

Baptisms

If you are reading this because you're planning to have a child baptized, then it's important that you read Chapter 5.

In the meantime, you may want to talk to the folks you are inviting to the baptism service. I've seen uncles show up feeling really uncomfortable in suits they haven't worn for years, and aunts feeling a little silly in an old, flowered hat and white gloves.

Tell them things have changed. Sure they can dress up if they want. It is, after all, a special occasion. But there's no dress code for friends and relatives at a baptism, any more than there is for a regular service. So just tell them to wear whatever is comfortable.

And tell them not to be surprised if they are asked to participate in a special way. Many United Church congregations and ministers include a question for families and friends of the person (child or adult) being baptized. It's a wonderful opportunity for them to publicly declare their love and support.

Baptism, in the United Church, is almost always during a regular service of worship.

Weddings

If there's a "dress code" at weddings, it comes from the expectations of the couple and their sense of how formal or informal

the wedding may be. If you're reading this because you're planning to get married in the United Church, make sure you read that all-important Chapter 5.

Meanwhile, as you are preparing, tell your friends and family that a wedding in a church is a service of worship. People popping up and down taking flash pictures or trying to get it all on smartphones don't support the attitude of reverence that should be part of the service of "holy matrimony." Usually the minister will gently tell folks when it's appropriate to take pictures.

Important! One of the very first things to do when you're working on arrangements and dates and stuff, is phone the church. Check with the minister. You could save yourself and the church a lot of hassle.

Religious language

I'm sure you've run into people who seem to use a lot of words and phrases like "Jesus" and "Hallelujah" and "Yes, Lord." You don't have to talk like that in the United Church. Not that there's anything wrong about that if it is genuine.

United Church people hardly ever use religious words. That's not a compliment. We really *should* learn how to talk about what we believe. Not doing so is one of our big weaknesses. But you don't need a specialized vocabulary to do that.

Many United Church folks are refugees from really uptight churches and they get squirmy when they hear what they sometimes call "Jesus talk." That bothers me. It seems to me that somewhere between "Jesus talk" and not talking about your faith at all (which is what mostly happens) there's got to be a happy medium.

I've got a lot to say about that in Chapter 6.

26

What do you have to believe?

You don't have to sign a paper or take a pledge or make any commitments when you come to a United Church.

Eventually, as you begin to feel more comfortable and have a sense of what the church is about, somebody will ask you to help out with some of the many things that happen in the life of a church. You're not required to do anything, but we hope that you'll want to get involved. And it's a great way to make friends.

The United Church is a "non-creedal" church. That means we don't say you have to believe this, or you can't believe that. When you boil it right down, what you believe is between you and God. I can tell you what I believe, but I can't tell you what you should believe.

Having said that, there are things we, as a church *do* believe. They're not nailed down tight like some of the traditional creeds, but they do reflect the centre of who we are.

That statement (in fact most of this chapter) is a bit over-simplified. So be sure to read Chapter 10.

Sunday school

One of the reasons many people come to church is because they want their children to have a religious education. A Christian experience.

There are many congregations in the United Church with very small, struggling Sunday schools. Lots of them have no Sunday school at all. They really need new people like you to join and stir things up a little. In other churches, the church school is alive and well and flourishing, but it may take many forms, and they don't all meet on Sunday.

Congregations grow when people get involved and then tell their friends and family about it. The next thing you know,

there's a lively church going with a bunch of kids around. If you want to know more about Sunday schools, read Chapter 4.

Laughing in church

Back in the "good old days," people never laughed in church. Or clapped. Now they do it all the time.

I don't think a Sunday goes by in our church that we don't have a chuckle over something. Occasionally folks are rolling in the aisles. Ministers often use humour in their sermons. And sometimes things get mixed up, and the best thing to do is to laugh.

On one occasion, when one of the ushers was bringing the offering plates down the aisle, he didn't quite watch where he was going and spilled the money all over the floor. As folks got down on their hands and knees to pick it all up, the minister said, "Well, for goodness sake, laugh!" Which we did.

Not long ago, I was reading the scripture lesson. Halfway through, I realized it was the wrong one. "Whoops!" I said. "I think I've just won the genius award."

All of us had a laugh, and I went on to read the right passage. There's lots more to say about laughing in church, and you'll find some of that in Chapter 2.

As for clapping – we don't usually applaud for things during a service of worship, though there's nothing really wrong with it. When the children's choir sings, we often clap. Or if there's something to celebrate. Sometimes we stomp our feet and clap our hands to some of the songs we sing.

I've seen people clap at the end of a particularly good sermon, but most ministers don't encourage it. A sermon, or an anthem by the choir, or anything else we do in the service, is not a performance. It is an offering – a way in which we praise God. And it just doesn't feel right to clap.

Apparently younger people may "live tweet" instead of clapping, and that it's worth five standing ovations. I don't even know what a "live tweet" is other than something that comes from an energetic canary.

Of course – as in every other public event – please turn off your cell phones. And it's not nice to be checking your e-mail during the sermon.

Phone and ask

There are lots of questions about our church that I can't answer. Questions about nursery care, Sunday school, parking, etc. have many different answers because every congregation is unique.

Many churches have a secretary who knows more about what is going on than the minister. Phone and ask. The secretary, or a volunteer answering the phone, will be delighted to explain things to you.

Lots of churches have websites, which may give you all the information you need. Search for the name of the church and the name of your community and see what you find.

Even better, if you know someone who already attends the church you are wondering about, buy them a cup of coffee and ask all the questions you like. Just remember that United Church folks are really just like you. None of us has all the answers. We're all trying to make sense out of life while we listen hard for God, who helps us as we stumble along. Join us, and learn as you grow!

Does it really matter?

Having written this whole chapter, I find myself wondering – does it really matter? Is all that stuff about sitting and standing and what to wear and who's who – really important?

Does it matter that I know the right words? Do I have to believe what I hear? Does it matter if I don't believe all the right things?

No, it isn't important. It really doesn't matter.

What *does* matter is that you open yourself to the free gift of grace – the gift of God's love. And even that can take a while. It took me a couple of years.

When all is said and done, your awareness of and response to God's unconditional love is the only thing that's important.

2

I'm Not Religious, But...

The Word became flesh and lived among us.
John 1:14

Having given you a quick look at the "nuts and bolts" of my church, let's back up to the beginning and start all over.

First of all, full disclosure.

The United Church of Canada is a wonderfully complex organism. Yes, organism. It looks like an organization from the outside, but when you're on the inside you realize there's something living and breathing about the whole thing. And like all living things, it has great beauty. And also its smelly spots.

Mostly I love the United Church. It is my church home, and I am describing it from the inside. But sometimes I get

pretty ticked off at it and I'm pretty ambivalent. I had thought of calling this book "Angels and Idiots," but some of my colleagues thought that might not be too wise.

Most often when I go to type "United Church" it comes out as "Untied Cruch." There must be some deep Freudian reason for that.

I love my United Church the way I love my family. Warts 'n all. But I'll try really hard to be honest.

Let me introduce myself

I'm 82 years old and still trying to figure out what "retirement" is all about. So far, all I've managed to eliminate is the paychecque, but not the work.

I'm married to Bev. She looks half my age, but actually she's only a couple of years younger. We had four kids, but now there are three. Lloyd, the youngest, took his own life years ago. The other three are all grown up, middle aged, and away from home. We have two absolutely wonderful grandchildren who have become fine adults of whom I am immensely proud. Don't let me get started because I can brag for hours.

Bev is a Rev. She's clergy. Retired.

I'm a layperson – a writer and storyteller by trade – and a founding partner of Wood Lake Publishing, which published this book. Wood Lake produces books and curriculum and other resources that are used by the ecumenical church community across North America, and even overseas. I've written a bundle of books, many of which are still available at the Wood Lake website or on Amazon.

If you want to know more about what Wood Lake does and what they publish, there's an address, phone number, and other information at the back of the book. Or go directly to the Wood Lake website: www.woodlake.com.

Strange credibility

I'm telling you this because my experience at Wood Lake played an immense role in forming in who I am and how I write. And because this book is the fourth edition of *This United Church of Ours*. It's become something of a classic, and a formative book for thousands of people in our denomination. Those first three editions were all bestsellers, but they are all badly dated. So if you see any of them around, put them in the recycling bin.

My time at Wood Lake taught me never to do that "pie-in-the-sky bye-'n-bye" stuff – predicting the end of the world at 12 noon on Tuesday (12:30 in Newfoundland).

Like me, you probably get a bit squirmy when people start using a bunch of hyper-religious words. It may surprise you, but most people in the United Church feel the same way. That's too bad, in a way, because to talk about religious things you need a few religious words. But very few! Not enough to scare anyone off or weigh you down.

Some people are really quite afraid of anything that sounds vaguely "religious." They prefer to talk about "spirituality," which of course is pretty much the same thing, except there's usually no community attached. For instance, when I go to meetings of writers or photographers, if the subject of religion comes up, they often say, "Well, I'm not religious, but ..."

It sounds as if not being religious is supposed to confer some kind of strange credibility. I don't mind if people have really thought it through and have decided that they are not religious, but I suspect most of them haven't. They just say it because they think it's expected.

My kind of God

Actually, many of my writer and photographer colleagues are really quite religious. But they're too gullible about much of

what they see on TV or the Internet or read in the papers. They think all Christians are like some TV evangelists, selling salvation during the day and sleeping around at night. Some of them think all Christians deny the science of evolution and still belong to the Flat Earth Society. Or they think of doddering old parsons drinking tea with doddering old ladies.

Or they say something like, "I don't believe in a God who zaps people when they do something wrong, or who hands out treats if you flatter him."

I don't believe in that kind of a god either! Neither do most of my friends in the United Church. When my writer and photographer colleagues hear that, we usually have a very different conversation. It often turns out they're hungry for something to believe in. But they've bought all the silly, sometimes insulting portrayals of church people they see on TV or read about in the press and social media.

Often, the only experience they've had of church and Christianity is a TV or movie caricature written by people who were children 30 years ago and who never went to Sunday school. It's people *my* age who remember Sunday school 60 or 70 years ago. They don't realize that, just like the rest of the world, the church has changed. Dramatically! That's why I'm updating this book for the fourth time in 30 years.

Plenty to answer for

If you get the conversation going far enough, you often find that people want to do something significant with their lives, and not just for bucks or prestige. Deep inside them there's a kind of hunger. They're not atheists. They just haven't taken the time to think through what kind of a god they believe in.

The fact is, genuine atheists are pretty scarce. Most people, even born-again atheists, have something, vague as it may be,

in that little mental compartment labelled "religion" or "spirituality."

Actually, more people go to church on a Sunday than go to sports events during the week. Check the web to find out how many churches are in your city. I counted 93 in Kelowna proper, which has a population of around 117,000. About 20 percent of Canadians are in church on any given Sunday, and of those, about 20 percent attend at least weekly.

Can you think of anything else 20 percent of the population participates in every week? Just because the popular media spend great gobs of time and money on sports and hardly any on religion simply means there's more money in sports.

Sports is all about conflict, one team or one person beating another team or person. The church is all about love and peace and justice, which is powerful stuff, but it doesn't make for action-filled dramas.

This is not to say that all those people going to church know why they go. And the folks who stay home may be very religious. Going to church and having an active, meaningful faith are not necessarily the same thing. As the evangelist Billy Sunday said, "going to church doesn't make you a Christian any more than going to a garage makes you a car."

It's true that organized religion has plenty to answer for. All religious groups, including my own United Church, have done some rotten things. Pointing the finger at religious leaders who have turned out to be crooks or charlatans or sexual deviants is sometimes necessary. And the media love it when they can salivate over a religious leader who has done something evil or just plain stupid.

With the mass media, as with all gossip (which much of it is), "viewer discretion is advised."

A little thought would help

But the fact that religious groups contain a few deadbeats doesn't discredit religion any more than deadbeats in politics discredit the whole democratic process, or irresponsible journalists prove all media to be unreliable.

Some of my friends in the writing business assume that if you close the door on religion you step into a wider world. You free yourself up for something better. Baloney! (I had a stronger word but the editor took it out.)

Okay, there's some truth in that charge. Some religious groups put their people into emotional and intellectual strait jackets, just as some political systems have done. The only way to be human is to break free.

But those groups and systems are aberrations. I hear about them from folks whom I think of as "refugees" from such religious groups. In the congregation where I worship, we have been immensely enriched by a dozen or more folks from the LGBTQ community, who have come from an exclusive religious group. They came to us looking for simple acceptance – a place where they can be who they are, like everybody else. They have felt unwelcome, sometimes insulted and marginalized, in other denominations.

Political systems and religious structures should serve people, not the other way around. A genuine faith sets you free. That's a basic principle behind all the world's great religions. In Christianity, it was expressed by Jesus who said, "I came that you might have life, in all its fullness."

The ache of loneliness

The late Margaret Laurence (a Canadian novelist of international renown) was a strong supporter and mentor to Wood Lake Publishing when I was involved in starting the company.

"Keep telling the story without all the crap that usually gets attached to it," she wrote to me, "because then I can give your books to my literary friends. They've got their lives all screwed up because the only thing they believe in is themselves, and that's just not enough." Margaret was a long-time member and supporter of the United Church.

I ache for Margaret's friends and for a number of my own friends who have the same attitude. So many, especially high-profile personalities, are terribly lonely people with lots of acquaintances, but no real friends. So often, they are hungering for the kind of friendship and sense of personal meaning that a Christian community can give. Or, at least, the Christian community as it's lived in denominations like the United Church. We're a long way from perfect in that department, but at least we are trying. Trying hard. Some people tell us we're too far ahead of the rest of the pack, but that depends on the congregation and the issue. Sometimes we're running to catch up.

Too many people have thrown their religion out because of something negative they vaguely remember from long ago. They may have left the church years ago because of some incident or comment. Or because they think high-pressure TV evangelists represent all denominations. Or because they heard or read something that was narrow-minded and perhaps even full of hate.

It's sad. Very sad.

Freedom!

Genuine religion frees you up. A cult ties you down. Some well-established and respectable groups are cults, I think.

The religious perspective that everything we do has meaning is certainly more liberating than the view of life that refuses to consider any questions or possibilities beyond the logical,

practical, survival view of life. For such people, if life has any meaning, it's so abstract and philosophical that it makes no significant difference.

To believe that humans are infinitely precious to a loving God is no harder than believing humans are simply organisms that function for a few years and then die. "You're born, you thrash around, then you die," is the way one cynic put it. True, maybe. But that kind of thinking puts no gas in my tank.

I respect people who thoughtfully and honestly reject religion. I also feel sorry for them. To abandon religion may be honest and honourable, but it isn't exactly leaping a prison wall.

If the kind of religion I'm talking about is a delusion, at least it's a delusion of grandeur and joy. If a lively faith is a delusion, at least it's a dynamic delusion, one that puts spice, zip, and fun into life.

If my religion is pure fantasy, it's a fantasy I can enjoy in the warmth of a spiritual community that accepts me the way I am. Warts and all.

So here I am, probably in the last decade of my life, with a pacemaker that keeps my heart beating and pills that keep my blood from clotting. I have a faith and a community that will see me gently into those final years, and support my loved ones when I'm gone.

I don't think that's just a pious delusion. But if it is, it's a lot better than the teeth-clenched, white knuckled "reality" so many people take to their graves.

If you know how to laugh

That's where I've ended up. That's not where I began. I began my adult life as a semi-militant atheist who would have begun conversations with, "I'm not religious myself, but…"

I worked as a news reporter and was sent to cover an event

at a local United Church. I was to do a story on a speaker, a "name" of some sort. The topic was of interest to church people presumably, though I couldn't have cared less.

Slowly, pushing past the green fog of my cynicism, the speaker got through to me. I remember him well. Not his name, but his jokes. They were good, spicy, gutsy stories and we all laughed until we literally ached. Then just as the laughter reached a peak, he burned a sentence into my consciousness.

"If we know how to laugh, then we also know how to pray. Let us pray!"

That man shattered my image of Christians. To suggest that laughter belonged in the church – that at some level laughter was like praying – didn't correspond at all with what I thought these people believed.

I was convinced Christians worshipped a stuffy grandfather in the sky whose chief joy was saying "Thou Shalt Not!" to just about anything that was fun.

That church basement event wasn't what you'd call a "conversion experience," but it was a tiny crack in my armour of distaste for anything vaguely connected with the church. From that point on, I listened just a bit more openly.

I began to realize I was operating on ideas about the church that had gone out with the *Ed Sullivan Show*. Since I had hardly ever gone to church as a child, I had little first-hand experience to go on. But I do remember what I thought was a photograph of God in an old Bible. It looked so real! God was sitting on a cloud, zapping sinners with thunderbolts.

Hidden back in my childhood memory were feelings of anger at a church that wanted my dad to stand up and make a public confession of his "sin," because he had grown a mustache. Apparently there's some obscure phrase in the Bible about that.

I also remember an evangelist coming to town. I must have been very small, but I can remember being afraid because he kept yelling and shouting.

What's going on around here?

I came into the United Church as an adult without any real church background. Within a year, I found myself an "elder." I was often terribly confused. Things everybody else seemed to know, I didn't. And I was too embarrassed to ask.

Since then, I've found that a great many people who join the church as adults are in the same situation. I worship at First United in Kelowna, British Columbia, as I've already mentioned. About half, maybe two-thirds of the congregation, is made up of older persons. Many churches are like that.

But there's also an enthusiastic batch of young families, and when it's children's time in the worship service, there's a couple of dozen ankle biters gathered around Cheryl Perry, one of our ministers.

There's also a bunch of unattached singles of various ages, and who knows what other kinds of configurations of people. We like to call ourselves a "Rainbow Community" because we are delightful bunch of people of various colours and convictions, ideas and lifestyles, as well as sexual orientations and gender expressions.

It's a fun bunch!

The covenant community

When I first joined the church, I discovered two things, and I have no idea which came first. I found some people who took an interest in me, who liked me even when I acted like a cocky, smartass kid. Through them, I began to sense what this God they worshipped was really like.

For me, there were no shattering "born again" experiences. Changes happened slowly over several years. But they happened. From a sense of aimlessness and frustration, I found a sense of knowing what life was about and what I should be doing with mine.

In other words, I found myself being part of a special kind of community called the church. This community has a history that goes back thousands of years. It includes people from almost every country in the world, yet it takes a very special form in a little faith community known as a congregation.

My congregation and the church as a whole has its "warts" just as I have. There are a few "saints" and a few "s.o.b.s," but the vast majority of us simply have strengths and weaknesses, good days and bad days. We're human.

Living in that human community, I experienced (which is different from learning or understanding) the truth that God loves us and yearns for us to love back.

Morning sickness

There was very little church life in my growing-up years. But in my late teens I did join a choir at a United Church in Lethbridge, Alberta, mainly because of a beautiful blond soprano. When that romance faded, so did my "commitment."

A romance that hasn't faded is the one I have with Bev. She grew up in church. Well, sort of. Her parents went mostly at Christmas and Easter. Shortly after we were married, she got talked into teaching Sunday school. (She wasn't a "Rev" then.)

Not many months later, she began suffering a not uncommon malady called morning sickness. She felt miserable till near noon. After that, she looked absolutely glorious. Since I had some responsibility for that morning sickness, I "volunteered" to substitute in the Sunday school.

But I had a problem. I considered myself an atheist. Well, at least an agnostic. There I was, in that dingy furnace room that doubled as a classroom, teaching an unruly gang of eight-year-old boys what I only half believed myself.

Actually, I had three problems. One was integrity. How do you teach stuff you don't believe? Another was sheer ignorance. I had never gone to Sunday school. Or church. Now, here I was teaching the stuff. My third problem was utter terror. Have you ever been alone in a furnace room with a gang of eight-year-old boys?

Dave Stone was our minister. "Why don't you join a Bible study group?" he asked. "Find out about that God you don't believe in."

I can't tell you the exact point at which it happened, but one day I knew I was a Christian. One day it started to make sense.

I'd always thought that religion would shut down my life. It would give me a bunch of rules that would take most of the fun out of living. Religion meant running away from real life.

Instead, it opened life up. The more I understood about that tiny seed of faith that seemed to be sprouting inside me, the more I felt open. Liberated. Free to look at my life and see what I wanted to do with it.

Not my grandchild!

"Mom," I said on the phone. "Sit down."

"What's wrong, Ralph?" she wanted to know. In those days you didn't phone long distance unless there was a disaster.

"Nothing's wrong, Mom," I said. "Bev and I are going to the Philippines as missionaries."

A long pause. "Are you crazy?"

"Yes, Mom, a little. But that's what we're doing. We're con-

vinced that's what God wants us to do."

"With a small baby? You're not taking my grandchild to some godforsaken jungle!"

"Oh, that's the other thing, Mom."

"What!" Mom sounded a bit panicky.

"Bev's pregnant again."

I won't tell you the rest of what Mom said, but let's just say she wasn't enthusiastic. We had similar conversations with most of our family and many of our friends.

We went to the Philippines and spent five wonderful, growing years there. Bev studied theology at the fine university where we lived (it was anything but a "godforsaken jungle") though she didn't become an ordained minister till many years later.

This new "opening up" of our lives then took us (there were now four children in the family) to live in an African-American community in New Jersey and to work for the National Council of Churches in a huge office building in New York City.

Coming home

Then, after ten years of living in other people's countries, we moved back "home." The first Sunday, we went to church. I remember thinking, "Canada may not be the best country and the United Church may not be the best church, but it's *my* country and *my* church." And I felt a deep sense of love for both.

On the other hand, the experience of living and travelling abroad also gave us a deep appreciation for many kinds of people and cultures, for different traditions and denominations. As people shared the beauty of what God had given them, Bev and I learned to appreciate our own roots even more.

We moved often in those early years. Each time we moved, we headed for a church where we knew we'd find friendship and acceptance – a place to belong.

Sometimes the Christian life seemed like such a long pilgrimage. We got fed up or angry at the way the church did some things and didn't do others. There were people in the church who let us down and people we let down. And some people we just plain didn't like.

But, when I look around, I can't see a better way. My Christian faith gives me a deep sense of joy and fulfillment. Life would be drab and meaningless without it. I don't know of any community in which I'd rather express this faith than in The United Church of Canada.

A very Canadian church

Many times in the Philippines and in the U.S., people asked me questions about the United Church of Canada. I couldn't always answer them. It would have been much easier for me to describe a Catholic or a Presbyterian.

It's hard to pin down what the United Church is. It doesn't have a clear-cut identity, but it certainly has some defining characteristics.

It's a Canadian church. A number of years ago, author John Robert Colombo said "the two most Canadian of institutions are the National Hockey League and the United Church of Canada." I'm not sure if he intended that as a compliment or as an insult, but regardless, it's not true any longer, for either the NHL or the United Church.

The United Church is Canadian in the way it sprang out of our desire to cooperate rather than compete on this harsh, northwestern frontier. The settlers, especially in those tiny western communities, knew it was either one church together, or no church at all.

The Methodist, Presbyterian, Congregational, and Union churches came together in 1925 to form The United Church of

Canada. The dream was that the various traditions would continue with their own unique way of doing things. It didn't work out that way. It didn't take long before it became homogenized into a single denomination.

The Evangelical United Brethren became part of our community in 1968. For a while, we had discussions with the Christian Church (Disciples) toward some kind of union, but nothing came of that. We had a courtship going with the Anglicans, too, but that didn't work out either.

For most of those years, we ignored First Nations people who were part of our community from day one. Their rich contribution is slowly beginning to dawn on us, enough that some indigenous symbolism has now been incorporated in our United Church crest. Visit the national church website (www.united-church.ca) to read the story and have a look.

Good days and bad days

The United Church has certain distinct characteristics. Words I'd use to describe them include freedom, openness, warmth, diversity, courage, and integrity.

That's on good days. On bad days I think we're really a gaggle of opinionated do-gooders mixed in with a large batch of wishy-washy fence-sitters.

Our greatest strength and our greatest weakness is the variety of viewpoints in one denomination. A dilemma and a blessing in one wrapping.

If we can be true to our heritage, the right and left wing of the church will learn to fly together. We won't always feel comfortable, but we'll listen to each other.

With respect! That means really listening and wanting to understand, not simply waiting for the other person to take a breath so you can jump in and set them right.

If we don't learn to do that, the United Church will lose one of its distinctive and, for me, essential characteristics. In fact, I think if we don't learn how to do that, we're lost. At best, we'll be dancing on one leg.

We are also an ecumenical church. "Ecumenical" is a Greek word we use when we're talking about the whole Christian church – all the denominations. The United Church has a long history of putting lots of time, energy, and money into ecumenical ventures, especially in working for justice here in Canada and overseas.

When we talk about justice in the United Church, we simply mean being fair and gentle with all of God's creation. Especially with people at the bottom of the economic and social ladder – in Canada and around the world.

I am very proud of my church in that regard. But recently, with budget constraints, the United Church (like all the other mainline denominations) found it necessary to cut back on their ecumenical commitments. Even so, we are still deeply involved with the ecumenical community, much of it through deeply committed volunteers. We're doing more than is immediately visible on the surface.

An open church

We are not a "confessional church." Although we have a creed, it's not something you have to say or sign before you can become a member. Nor do we demand that you use a certain set of religious words, or pray in a certain way, or believe in a particular interpretation of the Bible.

We *do* have convictions! We just don't believe in formulas. Faith is a living thing. And you can't dissect a living thing without destroying it.

Our creed expresses much of what our church people be-

lieve. We say it often together (search for "United Church of Canada A New Creed" on the national website: www.united-church.ca).

But it's just a statement. It has already been changed as the church changes. The most recent change was the addition of the phrase "to live with respect in Creation," a line that was included at the suggestion of some of our First Nations members. The creed may be changed again as our understanding of God keeps growing.

Most recently, we developed a longer document called "The Song of Faith," which you can also find on The United Church of Canada website. It's not so much a statement of what we believe as a beautiful and powerful poem that helps us imagine who we are as children of God.

More and more, we are trying to be an inclusive church, a community where everyone is valued and appreciated. That's why we also use the traditional creeds from time to time, such as the Apostles' Creed and the Nicene Creed. It's to connect ourselves to our Christian forebears who tried to put words around their faith. Christianity has been through huge changes since those early statements, but we look back with gratitude for the courage of our ancestors in the faith.

We do believe in a God who was revealed to us in the person of Jesus of Nazareth, and who is still revealed to us by the Holy Spirit. That part doesn't change.

Middle-class diversity

We are a middle-class church, both economically and educationally. Some people object when I say that, and I agree it may not be a good thing. But, it's true anyway.

The majority of United Church members are white, middle class, and complain about high taxes. But there are more and

more non-Anglo-Saxons in our church. There are people of every variety you could imagine.

That diversity extends all the way up through the organization and leadership of the church. The first layperson to be chosen Moderator was a very unconventional medical doctor named Bob McClure. The Moderator is the highest elected position in the church. That happened in 1968.

At that time, I wrote him a letter asking how we should address him, since traditionally Moderators were called, "Right Reverend," and he wasn't a "reverend." (We were more formal in those days.) His response? "Call me Bob."

One of our most beloved leaders during the 1980s was Sang Chul Lee, our Moderator from 1988–1990, who was a refugee from Korea.

Before that (1974), we elected Wilbur Howard, who is an African-Canadian. Stan McKay, a First Nations leader, was chosen as our Moderator in 1992. There have been a number of women who followed Lois Wilson. In 1980, she was the first woman to be elected as head of a major Canadian church. A few years ago, Gary Paterson was the first openly gay person to be elected as Moderator. Our current Moderator is Jordan Cantwell, the first openly lesbian person.

This diversity of the United Church becomes strength when we see the church as a mosaic, each different piece contributing to the colourful beauty of the whole.

Not only in our church, but in our country, we've simply got to learn to live creatively with such diversity. Jesus emphasized a genuine love for those who have different traditions or ways of worshipping God. "In God's house, there are many rooms," he told us.

The challenge is to learn to live Jesus' words, "love your neighbour" and "love your enemy." Sometimes, they're the same people and often they sit next to us in church.

Part of the problem is that we often sentimentalize "love." Love, as projected by our culture, is two people gazing into each other's eyes and finding there a perfect reflection of themselves. Those of us who have struggled with the problems of love within a marriage, family, and church know that real love means living creatively with the differences. Real love always means commitment, conflict, forgiveness, and reconciliation. And respect! Real love is a choice! That's hardest and most important with the people closest to us.

Many kinds of people

Because we have such a variety of people in the United Church, there's a real temptation to set up categories. I guess I need to do a bit of that so I can describe some of the kinds of folks that make up our community. Please don't take my labels too seriously.

One group is often called the "social activists" or "liberals." They don't use many religious-sounding words, but claim their faith should be evident in the way they live. They are very critical of the social scene; of large corporations, governments and trading practices that discriminate against poor people, or that harm our non-human relations and the environment we all share.

These social justice Christians (of which I am one) are often criticized for being entirely too comfortable with society's general beliefs on such matters as sex. We can be very judgmental, sometimes arrogant, about people who don't agree with us.

But these "liberals" have also been hugely instrumental in bringing about needed social change. Without this social justice emphasis, the church would be in danger of degenerating into a kind of feel-good supper club.

Others get tagged as "evangelicals" or "conservatives." They

often quote from the Bible and are very concerned about personal morality, often about matters related to sex. They are quite comfortable using religious language and showing enthusiasm in worship. They're often faulted for accepting the social order uncritically and failing to see their part in the sin of an oppressive world order. They, too, can be very judgmental, sometimes arrogant, about people who don't agree with them.

But they also remind us of where we came from, and where it is that we get the spiritual courage, the gas in the tank, to help us live the Christian life. They are often the most active people in the local congregation.

The good news is that the "liberal" and "evangelical" people are beginning to listen to each other, and that'll be good for all concerned.

There are some groups and individuals in the church who emphasize meditative prayer. Others have a strong appreciation for the sacraments and symbols of worship. United Church people have learned much from the Anglican and Roman Catholic traditions about this.

There are those who bring together their understanding of Christianity and psychology in order to understand themselves and others better. Some have looked toward the New Age movement for ways to enrich their Christian understanding.

There are many people in our church who simply want to get along with everybody. Their motto is "don't rock the boat," avoid troublesome questions, and let's just all get along.

Personal and social

Every group in the church, like any gathering of people, has its strengths and weaknesses. In some circles of the United Church, there are people willing to look beyond the labels, beyond the caricatures, and recognize that they have the most to learn from

people with whom they disagree. The church has an almost desperate need for more of such people.

More of us are trying to take our personal, biblical faith and social responsibility more seriously. We're trying to be more enthusiastic and open in the expression of our faith. And we want to be more conscious of how we live this faith in the social and political world.

We'd like to think of ourselves as "evangelical" in the sense that we're enthusiastic about sharing the good news and "fundamentalist" in that we try to focus on biblical fundamentals, the essentials of faith. We'd like to be "liberal" in the sense of being open to new ideas and "social radicals" in that we don't walk away from tough issues of justice, liberation, and the care of God's creation. And "conservative" in wanting to preserve what is the best and most relevant in our rich tradition.

Unfortunately, some United Church members are not very clear what their faith stance is. What's worse, they're not motivated to do the work involved in finding out. They are poorer for it.

But, as a whole, the United Church is constantly examining itself – its mission and what it believes. We invite people from other denominations and from other parts of the world to come and tell us what they see. We try to listen hard to hear and benefit from what they say.

Sometimes their comments are negative – sometimes we're really flattered. Not long after the United Nations said Canada was the second best country in the world in which to live, Bishop John Shelby Spong (a very controversial figure in the U.S. Episcopal Church) said the United Church was the best denomination in North America. A similar compliment came from Fr. Matthew Fox, a radical Catholic priest who moved over into the U.S. Episcopal church in 1993.

Some were delighted by these comments. Others, considering where the remarks came from, felt they were less than complimentary.

The Bible can be trusted

It's all very well to say, "The Bible is our authority. I'll read it and I'll know which way to go." But people interpret the Bible in so many ways. Every Christian sect and all the many denominations find their justification in the Bible. In the Bible study groups that meet in many churches, there are as many ways of looking at the scripture as there are people.

In those Bible study groups, as in the church as a whole, a few still rely on the traditional King James version of the Bible, with its "thee" and "thou," and other Shakespearian language. Most people use one of the many modern translations and paraphrases. It's good to hear these ancient truths and timeless stories expressed with various wordings.

I've always felt that the Bible can be trusted, provided we see it whole and don't pick out a phrase here and a sentence there to justify what we've already decided. Many of us would like to see the church spend more time with the Bible, especially learning some of the powerfully rich stories of people struggling to hear the authentic voice of God in their lives.

Shalom

There's no single word that describes United Church people. Sometimes, we are simply a pious do-gooder non-profit organization and we really have very little reason for being.

But when we are what God calls us to be, the only word that comes close to describing us comes from Hebrew: *shalom*.

Shalom is often translated as "peace," but it's a far richer word. It means more than peace as the absence of conflict. *Sha-*

lom has within it the concept of wholeness, of a yearning for justice, of hope, of unity, of common purpose, of prosperity. It's a very rich word and you'll find it used often by United Church people.

The word *shalom* helps us know we are not alone. Others have been on this journey before us – centuries of searching people stumbling along life's journey – Abraham and Sarah, Mary and Joseph, Nellie McClung, Desmond Tutu, Sang Chul Lee, Marion Best, Nelson Mandela, and Anna Williamson.

Anna Williamson? She's a person in our congregation who very quietly, in a hundred different ways, simply does what needs doing. Anna would be surprised and very embarrassed to see her name in this book because she's not doing "anything special." So that's not her real name, but she is a very real person.

In the church as a whole there are thousands of people like Anna. We call them "the company of saints." They're not a group of "perfect" people. But, through the centuries, they are the ones who have discovered a pathway.

A pathway

We begin our journey of faith expecting to be alone on the road, sort of hoping for a little "divine guidance" along the way. Then, we find that most of our "divine guidance" comes through very ordinary folk we find walking beside us.

These are the saints in blue jeans and sneakers who help us over the rocks and who bandage our bruised knees – people we call "the church."

We walk together with others in our shalom community, which extends way beyond the United Church and includes people from other faith traditions.

Perhaps most important, we discover Jesus there, too; walking among us, walking beside us.

3

Sunday Morning

*They devoted themselves to the apostles' teaching and fellowship,
to the breaking of bread and the prayers.*
Acts 2:42

So what do we actually do in a typical United Church on Sunday morning? Well, there's no such thing as a typical United Church. If I tried to explain all the variations and combinations of Sunday worship, I'd write an encyclopedia, and a dull one at that.

What follows is the compromise.

Exceptions

No matter what I might say about the United Church, there are always exceptions. A number of congregations are feeling their way into this age of computers and iPhones and the Internet by experimenting with different kinds of music, different kinds of worship, and different ways of reaching out to the community. More and more lay people are stepping up and helping to lead

worship, and their contributions include new ideas. As with all new things, they encounter mixed reactions.

What follows are descriptions of various United Church communities. None of them actually exist. Each is an amalgam of several congregations. Any real congregation would combine features of several of these, plus a few that are uniquely its own. And you may find yourself in a United Church that is trying something totally new, which could be really wonderful or sensationally awful.

Try not to jump to conclusions on the basis of a single church experience. You don't know what a job is like by working one day, and you don't really know what a church is like by attending just one service. Try half a dozen.

Changing needs

Just as business and industry have developed consultants who study and make recommendations on corporate culture, organization, and methods, etc., the mainline churches have spawned a variety of folks who try to help us become more relevant to the changing needs of society. They travel around doing various workshops, which sometimes are very helpful and sometimes simply raise our anxiety levels. I mention this because there's a good possibility you'll encounter some experiments in worship at any church you go to. If they ask for feedback and you have some feelings about it, express them.

But don't expect the church to be like the one you may remember from your childhood. Don't expect old, old hymns and long, long prayers. Things have changed!

In fact, things have been changing more rapidly in the last few years than ever before. It is my impression that there is more diversity among congregations than ever. No two are exactly alike. But these fictitious descriptions might help.

Dover Park United

There are two services each Sunday at Dover Park United. The first one is at 9:30 a.m., the second at 11:00. They are identical, except that the people tend to be younger at the first service. The church is full, but not packed. And there are a lot of young families.

The Rev. Dawson Peterson is 40ish with graying hair. He and the choir walk casually into the sanctuary, which is buzzing with muted conversation behind the quiet music of a large electric organ. Nobody pays too much attention. Folks are too busy catching up with their friends.

The choir sits down in the pews, Peterson pins a small lapel mike to his tie, tucks the cord behind the jacket of his suit, looks up at the congregation and says, "Hi." Many people in the pews respond with "Hi," or "Good morning."

"Does anybody have a song or hymn they'd like to sing this morning?" he asks.

"Number 509" comes a quick response from someone who was obviously ready. Everyone sings "I, The Lord of Sea and Sky" from *Voices United*, the more or less standard United Church hymn book. That's not surprising. According to *The United Church Observer*, it's at the top of our denominational hit parade. Or at least it was. These things change.

Peterson then talks about events coming up in the congregation that week. The Stewardship Committee had a garage sale and Elena Dowds stands up to tell people the sale was a success. She's given a round of applause. Then several committee meetings are announced.

There are always half a dozen visitors and new people at the services, so Peterson asks them to identify themselves and he welcomes them. Everybody claps.

The children are beginning to get fidgety, but the service is ready to begin.

There's a "Call to Worship," a kind of introduction to the service. It's shown on the video screens that are strategically located around the sanctuary. That's followed by another hymn. This time it's one of the "classic" favourites: "Joyful, Joyful, We Adore You!"

Then there's a prayer and a reading from one of the psalms from *Voices United*, though it's all shown on the video screens. The congregation reads the lines printed in bold and sings a one-line response when the bold letter "R" comes up.

As the psalm ends, the children begin to move to the front of the church. Peterson leaves the pulpit and motions to the rest of the children to follow. Soon they're all sitting together on the steps leading up to the front of the church.

The image on the video screen switches to a live camera focused on Peterson and the children. That's so the congregation can see the pictures or objects Peterson often uses. Some adults say they get more out of the children's time than out of the sermon.

Sometimes Peterson has a story for the children. Sometimes he asks them questions. Unlike the adults in the church, the children don't hesitate. If they have something to say, they say it. Peterson used to treat the youngsters as "adults in training." Now, he sees them as full members of the church with their own gifts and riches to share.

Peterson's change in attitude came through a church school curriculum called *Seasons of the Spirit*. This curriculum encourages congregations to see children as full participating members of the church with their own gifts and talents to share. It makes quite a difference to the style and content of the service.

That curriculum bases its lessons on the Bible readings as-

signed for that day from the lectionary, the same readings that are recommended for the morning worship service.

The lectionary (used by many denominations) is a schedule of Bible readings, spanning three years. Over any given three-year period, the people at Dover Park will hear most of the major readings from the Bible. Peterson bases his sermons on those readings because, he says, "it keeps me from riding my own hobby horses."

"Besides," he adds with a grin, "there are really good preaching resources that have all kinds of neat stories and ideas to go with the lectionary. Sermon preparation time is cut in half."

All together now!

After the children's "theme conversation," comes a song. It's "intergenerational," which means that it's selected with the children in mind. This morning the song is, "I Am the Light of the World," a bouncy tune, which the organist drags a little.

The children leave during the last verse of the song. And the church looks strangely empty without them.

Marj Cornelson also leaves her seat and by the time the last child has left she's ready to read the day's scriptures. Marj has two children in the church school. She knows they'll work on the same Bible readings in their classes, but probably in the form of stories, songs, and activities.

Now, it's time for the choir. There are about 20 members, wearing bright maroon robes. No one in the choir is paid, except the organist who is also the choir director. She gets a small honorarium. The choir sings an anthem called "The Lord Is My Shepherd," based on Psalm 23. Musically, that would probably fall in the category of a "popular classic."

The choir sits and the minister stands up. It's time for the sermon. Twenty minutes.

If there is such a thing as a "typical" United Church sermon, Peterson preaches it. It's not what you'd call "evangelical," though he talks often of spiritual growth and the "life in Christ." It's not what you'd call a social justice sermon either, though he often relates some of the scripture to current issues of justice and equality. It's a well-thought-out meditation, and the people find it interesting, and, like most of his sermons, very often useful and relevant to the things they face in daily life.

The sermon ends with a short prayer and a song. This time it's from a coil-bound book called *More Voices* and it's a lively piece called, *It's a Song of Praise to the Maker*. Most people sing from the words on the video screens, but a few use the book because they like to have the notes as well as the words.

The song is followed by the "pastoral prayer" in which Peterson tries to express some of the concerns he has been hearing from people throughout the week. He also puts in some of the things that bug him personally.

When the plates are passed around for the offering, it is not just a matter of gathering money so the church can operate. The offering is the congregation's response to God's love. It's a special way for them be part of the church's outreach program. The offering is followed by the last hymn and the benediction, which is the final blessing before people leave.

Peterson stands at the door shaking hands with everyone. He doesn't particularly like doing this, because so many people all at once turn into a blur for him. He's told them many times, "Don't say anything to me on the way out on Sunday morning that you expect me to remember." They do anyway.

Dover Park has a good-looking building with a high vaulted, laminated beam roof, and lots of windows. People admire the architecture, but those who sit on the Building Committee know what it costs to heat all that space. Others worry about green-

house gas emissions. "We'd make a better statement to the community if we had a batch of solar panels on the roof," some members have been saying.

The people of Dover Park also worry about the heavy upkeep costs. Sometimes they find themselves resenting the heavy financial burden and wonder out loud if they are "overbuilt."

The building went up in the late '50s when it was assumed that Dover Park would be serving a huge area and financing would not be a problem. Old-timers in the church remember the high morale and enthusiasm that went with the building program and feel a little hurt by newcomers who can only see the high maintenance costs and energy leaks.

During the '60s the congregation went into a slump. But with a recent housing boom, attendance is up and the church's future looks reasonably bright.

Southhill United

Six kilometres south of Dover Park another congregation meets in a school gymnasium. There are no pews. People sit on stacking chairs. There seem to be kids everywhere. Some sit quietly, others act like kids. Over in the corner is an activity table where the young fry gather to colour or do other crafts. There's a chair nearby for a grandmother or other adult who tries to keep things down to a dull roar.

Except for two large banners near the front of the gym and the portable pulpit, it looks more like parents' day at the elementary school than a Sunday morning at church. But it's a regular congregation that calls itself Southhill United Church.

Joyce Nai-Chen is the minister. She wears a bright golden, ankle-length gown and a liturgical stole, both hand-woven by a member of her congregation. She moves around the hall, talking to this person and that. When she sees that the choir has

settled itself in the group of chairs near the front, she moves in that direction.

There's a teenager operating a laptop computer that controls a video projector, which throws an image onto the screen set up just to the left of the pulpit. The whole worship service has been put into *Power Point*. The teenager touches a button on the computer and the "Call to Worship" appears on the screen. Everyone says it together.

"The traditional word for worship is 'liturgy,' which means 'the work of the people,'" says Joyce. "It's something we all do together."

Doing things together seems to be a major characteristic of this congregation. A teenage boy reads the scripture, stumbling over some of the words. The "sermon" is a dialogue and a poem prepared by the young adults group. The announcements are made by people popping up here and there. In fact, Nai-Chen acts more like an MC or a coordinator than what you might generally think of as a minister. She likes having people involved.

There is no organ in this church, but there is a piano and a small instrumental group that plays soft rock versions of some of the hymns and that most Sundays performs a contemporary piece. The teenagers think it's great. Some of the older folks think it's loud, but they're glad it's there. "Not everything has to be geared to our tastes," says grey-haired Angus Tuttle. "There's something for everyone, but not everything is for everyone."

One of the hymns, found in *More Voices* but projected onto the screen, is "O Beautiful Gaia," which some folks find "entirely too new age." Others are glad the church is "finally catching up to some of the new language of contemporary spirituality." In any case, they all sing it together.

The choir doesn't wear gowns. They've talked about that

occasionally, but nobody wants them badly enough. There always seem to be more important things to spend their money on. When they stand up to sing, a child leaves her mom in the fifth row to join her dad in the choir. She stays there for the rest of the service and nobody seems to notice. A young mother opens her blouse and nurses her baby. Nobody pays attention to that either.

Like Dover Park, Southhill emphasizes small groups in the church. Both Nai-Chen and Peterson, at Dover Park, feel that Sunday morning worship should be a bringing together – a "celebration" of what happens during the week. And plenty happens during the week.

A connected sermon

There are several study groups at Southhill. One of them is a Bible study that looks at the lectionary readings coming up each Sunday. "We get so much more out of the worship service when we do this," they say.

The clergy find it useful, too. "It helps me hear what's on their hearts and minds," says Nai-Chen. "And that informs my sermon."

"People who don't get involved in the mid-week groups just don't get as much out of church," she continues. "The Sunday morning group is too big and there's no way you can feel you're a part of what's happening if that's all you plug into."

It's definitely a middle-class church. Most of the Southhill people own homes or condominiums, though they are heavily mortgaged. Many are business or professional people. They are generally well-educated and ambitious, and probably more in debt than they'd like to be.

Many of the people at Southhill have little church background or experience. In fact, about half the Board are not

even United Church members, which is technically against the regulations, but they do it anyway. They have little knowledge of the church and its traditions, and even less about the Bible and what it teaches. Their biggest asset is their eagerness to ask questions.

"I'm not worried about the lack of tradition," says Nai-Chen. "We're building traditions of our own. But I *am* worried about the lack of understanding of what their faith is all about. They're an easy mark for just about anyone who comes along and spouts a good, sincere-sounding line, including crackpots. We need to do far more Bible study, and I don't just mean learning a few verses here and there. I mean some solid, in-depth, progressive stuff. There are lots of people around who can quote isolated bits, but who miss the Bible's overall message of peace, justice, love, and community."

A continuing discussion (sometimes an argument) at Southhill is whether they should put up their own building. One committee drew up elaborate plans for a high-rise that would be a senior citizens' villa, a daycare centre, a community centre, and a church all rolled into one. They claimed they could get provincial and federal funding for such a venture, pointing to other congregations that have done this. They are the ones who feel that worshipping in a school just doesn't "feel like church."

Other members of the congregation point to the mind-boggling expense of building. "Let's buy a house or something," they say, "just so we can have an office for the minister and a place for small groups. But let's not get ourselves tied down by all the expense and fuss of a building."

Nai-Chen is very much on the side of the second group. "We can be the church without a building," she says. "It lets the church be the church. The people of God. We can respond to

64

the needs of each other and the community, instead of taking care of facilities."

Riverside United

Riverside United Church has a slightly older building than Dover Park. It's about the same size, with about the same number and kinds of people.

Harold Murphy, the minister, wears a sport jacket without a tie. He's among the congregation while they gather, smiling, laughing, and hugging. Murphy makes a fuss over newcomers, asking where they're from, introducing them to the people next to them in the pews. And he says a short prayer for them.

He begins the service with a fervent prayer. Very soon, a few hands are raised, palms upward.

During the sermon, Murphy refers to the Bible often and quotes from it. For him, the Bible is the ultimate and final authority. His sermons are emotional and usually last about 35 minutes, which is long for the United Church.

During the prayer following the sermon, Murphy leaves time for others to pray out loud, and several do. The singing is lively and includes a number of "choruses," songs specifically designed for easy group singing. The words are shown with a video projector. The congregation clearly enjoys these. The hymn book in the pews is not *Voices United* or *More Voices*, but one from a more conservative denomination.

The service is longer than at most United Churches, but few people complain. There's much handshaking at the door as people leave. Folks seem to be very friendly.

Riverside and Murphy represent the evangelical side of our United Church. They sometimes feel shut out of other parts of the church. Unfortunately, there's some reality behind that feeling. It's much easier to be inclusive with folks on the other side

of the world, than with members of your own family. It's hard being a minority group in a large organization.

When he arrived two years ago, Murphy appeared to have instant success. Many new people were joining the church. Still, in spite of newcomers, the congregation grew very little. Many of the old members had drifted to other congregations because they simply didn't feel comfortable with his emotional style of ministry. But Murphy attracted people from other United Church congregations and even other denominations – people who found something they needed in his highly charged preaching.

First United

In the centre of the city, you'll find First United Church. A few blocks away is Central United. One was a Methodist Church before union in 1925, the other was Presbyterian. Both are imposing structures that can seat many people. Both have large pipe organs. First United doesn't have a choir, but they have a skilled organist and four soloists. All are paid.

There are two ministers at First United. The "senior" minister preaches the sermons. That's Dr. Henry Guthrie, and he's expected to spend plenty of time on those sermons. He does, and they are well-researched models of what good sermons should be. Unfortunately, not enough people hear them.

Guthrie is assisted by Rev. John Madson, who visits in hospitals and the homes of the elderly. He's called the "visiting minister" and he usually reads the scripture on Sunday mornings.

When Guthrie enters the church for Sunday worship, everybody stands up. He wears a black academic gown and a professionally embroidered stole.

The congregation is sparse and mostly quite old, though here and there you can see a younger person in the rows of dark oak pews.

Everything proceeds according to the order in the printed bulletin. There are no screens or projectors. The four soloists sing the Lord's Prayer and a choral "Amen" after all the spoken prayers.

As people leave, many simply shake the minister's hand and say nothing. A few will say, "Good morning, Reverend."

First United would be in serious financial difficulty if it weren't for money left in wills by former members. And the church still has on its rolls some of the old moneyed families of the city, who come through whenever there's a financial crunch.

But First United, old and tired as it seems, is a church with a vision. They are well along on their plans to tear down their venerable old building. It will be very hard to see it go, because the walls seem to carry the memory, the *spirit* of all the faith and hard work that has made the church the force for good that it has been.

Nevertheless. "We've made the hard decisions," says an elder of this fine old church for more than half a century. "We'll carry enough of the symbols – the pulpit and the plaques and the stained-glass windows – into the new structure that will keep us in touch with our heritage."

The new structure will be a multi-storey, low-cost, energy-efficient housing complex, most of it intended for use by seniors. There'll be a smaller, more compact church on the ground floor, and office space for doctors, pharmacists, and other services that seniors might need.

Says Dr. Guthrie: "We have a ministry for and with seniors. That's our calling. We'll minister to the seniors now in our congregation, and to the many others – some of them in terrible poverty – who live in this downtown core."

Central United

Central United looks very much like First United. But you sense something very different. There's an ethnic mix here, something we're beginning to see more frequently in our denomination. There are several African Canadians, a few East Indians, and people of various Asian backgrounds scattered among the predominantly Anglo-Saxon congregation. Over on one side is a group of young women, and here and there a few young men. There are even a few kids.

The first thing you'll notice is that there's an interpreter signing everything that happens for the deaf persons in the congregation. There are large video screens at a number of key locations.

The folks at Central decided they would be inclusive, and they meant it. They became an "Affirming Congregation," which is another way of saying that gay, lesbian, bisexual, and transgendered people are not just welcome – the congregation openly celebrates who they are and the gifts they bring. They can participate in every aspect of the life of the church. Several Central United members are active in "Affirm United," an organization that offers community and support to LGBTQ people in our church (Google "Affirm United").

Central United has two ministers. The preaching minister is George Allison. Some people call him "Doctor," but most call him "George." Although he was not required to do so, when George was called to Central United, he told the search committee that interviewed him that he was gay.

"So what?" said Katheryn Parkinson, chair of the committee. Katheryn is a lesbian with a partner, who is also active at Central.

George's sexual orientation has never been an issue in the congregation. "He's not a 'gay minister,'" said Donna Popovsky,

who is also on the ministerial staff. "He's a minister who happens to be gay."

Donna and George are a ministry team. Some people think George is the "senior" minister, but in reality they have equal standing, though different responsibilities. Donna takes the lead in "outreach and education" for the congregation. It's Donna's work with young mothers that has brought a bunch of young families into the church.

Demographics

Both Central and First were built early in the 1900s and began as neighbourhood churches – one Methodist, the other Presbyterian. Many of the worshippers walked to services. "Church" was the centre of their community life. When those two denominations plus the Congregationalists and the Union Churches formed The United Church of Canada in 1925, there was some talk of combining Central and First, but since both congregations were strong and vigorous, the idea was never seriously discussed.

As the years passed, the original members of the congregation died or moved out of the immediate area. People from other traditions and cultures moved into the neighbourhood, replacing the primarily middle-class population who still referred to the British Isles as "the old country."

After World War II, thousands of people moved to the suburbs. Paved roads, the automobile, and a higher standard of living helped accelerate the trend. Soon the majority of First and Central members were driving ten to 30 kilometres from home to church.

Then, both congregations suffered the loss of ministers who had been there for several decades: one through death, the other through retirement. Many members, who had a deep loyalty to

their ministers but who were beginning to feel the burden of the long trek back and forth, decided to transfer their membership to a suburban congregation closer to home. Some simply dropped out altogether, as church going became less common in the 1960s and 1970s.

Both congregations found themselves hearing the empty echoes of a huge, unused building. Again there were suggestions that First and Central should be combined and one of the buildings sold. Property in the downtown core was worth a bundle. But the people making the suggestion underestimated the tenacity of the old but powerful people of both congregations, who had huge emotional investments in the buildings.

A call to the future

Those conversations didn't result in the combining of the two churches, but it *did* get the folks thinking seriously about their mission and their future.

The members of First United are excited about their building plans and their ministry with and for seniors.

Some of the people at Central are excited, too. It took planning, convincing, even a bit of arm-twisting, but the Board (the core governing body of the church) brought in a consultant who helped them take a hard-nosed look at their future. They decided that since they were in the downtown core, they would serve the downtown core.

Donna Popovsky was called to join the ministry because she had a sense of what a downtown congregation could be like and she had the skills to make things happen.

Now, several years later, with the help of some money from the national United Church, Central operates a daycare centre for working mothers, a clothing depot, and a food bank for people in need. Every Tuesday and Thursday morning, several dozen homeless women and men crowd into the hall for cof-

fee, sandwiches, and often some helpful counselling from Donna.

There are various programs for single parents and an active counselling program for people with particular problems, such as domestic violence or AIDS or substance abuse. Donna often goes to bat for the street people that come into the church looking for help, occasionally going with them to court to help ensure that justice is done.

Attendance is up on Sunday morning though not by much. Many members are developing a sense of mission and involvement. Some are still angry and suspicious. A few have left.

Central has stopped drifting. It has defined a role for itself and its future. If they go under, they'll do so knowing that, while they may not have been successful, they were at least faithful.

And the reality is that Central may well go under. The people in the congregation tend to be at the bottom of the income scale, and many are unemployed. At one time Central received some funding from the national United Church, but with budgets shrinking at all levels of the church, they are now on their own.

The situation does not look promising.

Korean United

There are actually two congregations at Central. Each Sunday morning a small congregation gathers in Central's spacious lounge. A worship centre is set up, and a small cluster of people gather.

Many of the congregation are elderly and, for them, the minister speaks in Korean. But there are also a number of young families gathered. In a few instances, one member of the family is not Korean. Some families don't use the Korean language very much in the home. So the service is conducted in English

as well, with the minister moving easily between both languages.

People don't seem to mind hearing the scriptures read in both Korean and English. "I like it," says Eileen Cho. "I understand the scripture more deeply when I hear it read in both languages."

A frequent subject of the sermons is the situation in Korea. There's concern for a divided country, about the dictatorship in the north, and fear that war may again break out between the two Koreas.

After the service, the congregation quietly puts everything away and leaves. The others at Central hardly know they are there.

Aspen Lake United

If you head down the parkway a dozen kilometres and turn east, you'll find Aspen Lake United Church. It's a small white building with a steeple too tiny for its size. A few years ago, it was one of four churches served by a single minister. A handful of families who remembered "the good old days" were keeping it open. But just barely.

Now, the church is full on Sundays. There's a thriving Sunday school and they have a part-time minister, the Rev. Muriel Clark.

Aspen Lake Church lives in the urban shadow. It used to be "way out of town," and ranchers and farmhands populated its pews. But farms became more mechanized and larger. Fewer people lived in the area until a few farms were subdivided into five- and ten-acre lots, and "hobby farmers" began to move in. The city suburbs, meanwhile, crept to within three kilometres of its door.

Few of the city people living in the countryside came to Aspen Lake Church until Clark was asked to come and fill in.

"Just Sunday services, that's all," she was told.

For Clark, that wasn't enough. She began visiting and phoning and making contacts. Gradually, some of new families appeared and they brought others. As they did, the character of the church changed. Most of the old families were still there, but the active nucleus was soon made up of younger, urban people who happened to be living in the country.

Aspen Lake Church is at that critical phase. It is getting too big to be a small church, and it is still too small to be a big church. Their assets include a prize piece of land, plenty of enthusiasm, and lots of potential.

One thing that bothers them is the possibility of losing the intimate community they have formed. Everybody knows everybody and the minister can call each person by name. When there's a church function, it's a family event, with the kids and everybody there.

Even the worship services have that "country family" flavour, though with a bit of "high-tech" spice. There's no music leader, so Clark uses an electronic hymn book, *Sing Hallelujah.* "We get to sing with the best musicians in the United Church. They're up there on the video screen. Works like a charm!" (You can find it on www.woodlakebooks.com.)

People enjoy the chatter and gossip before church and over coffee afterwards. Clark greets people at the door as they come in and seems to have something to say to each one of them.

The bulletins, when they have bulletins, aren't typed very neatly. Clark, in spite of her considerable talents, is a terrible typist, and there's no church secretary.

Unlike in some city congregations, people seldom "dress up" for church. As one member said, "Out here, going 'formal' means putting on a clean pair of blue jeans."

Cross Lake United

There's a special flavour to the service at Cross Lake United. The people gather around the fire in the box stove warming themselves against the chill from outside. They talk about the weather and the need for repairs on the church.

There is much laughter, and people share their stories as they share themselves. They talk about the fact that many of the local people are not coming to church lately and wondering how they could encourage them. But the church is still full for special celebrations like weddings, baptisms, wakes, and funerals.

Before the service begins, George Derrick, his brother Don, and several other friends plug in and tune up their electric guitars, and they begin to sing choruses they each know by heart, having heard them all their lives – songs such as "I'll Fly Away," or "Amazing Grace."

The minister is Aileen Garrioch, an indigenous woman who is studying at a special centre for First Nations ministers. Part of the service is in the Cree language of this First Nation, which someone translates into English. Part of it is in English and someone translates that into Cree. The Bible is read in both languages.

The small community knows that a special gift is being shared. There is a unique way of worshipping here, a way of viewing the Creator and the Christ. They feel it as they hear the words that are spoken and the songs that are sung.

Near the end of the service, the musicians take charge, and invite various members of the congregation to come forward and offer a personal testimony, make prayer requests of the congregation, or sing a favourite song or hymn. Sometimes people respond by gathering around the person who has spoken; they place their hands gently on that person's head or shoul-

der, and offer prayer. Sometimes people pray from the pews.

In some, but not all, indigenous United Churches, traditional native spiritual practices and teachings are beginning to find their way into the worship services. Smudging, for instance.

Oroville United

An hour's drive beyond the Aspen Lake church, down a winding country road, is the town of Oroville, and right in the middle of town is the old, red brick United Church.

It's the largest congregation in what's known as a "three-point charge." "That's because the minister has to 'charge' from one point (church) to another, every Sunday morning," jokes Marie Henderson, the Church Council Chair. Services are held at 9:00 in the morning at Caustia, and at 11:00 in Oroville. Othello, the other "point," has services on the first Sunday evening of each month.

Every Sunday morning finds the same group of people in Oroville and Caustia. Visitors are rare. The pews are about two-thirds full, which means 30 people in Oroville and 15 in Caustia. While there's a lively group of children in Oroville, there are seldom any in Caustia.

Small pastoral charges often have financial problems. Some wouldn't be open at all if it were not for help that comes through the Mission and Service fund of the national United Church, but that money seems to be rapidly drying up. Oroville-Caustia received aid from the Mission and Service fund until a few years ago when, after some hard work and dedication, they became self-sufficient, and now even contribute a little to that fund.

The Oroville-Caustia Pastoral Charge is run by a small group of people who accepted responsibility for it years ago. Sometimes they serve on committees and sometimes not, but every-

body knows who makes the decisions, and how. It seldom happens at meetings. Decisions are made informally and by the time the meetings come around everybody knows what will happen.

Everybody, that is, except the minister. At the moment, it's Rev. Anne-Marie Dexter. This is not only her first church, it's also her first experience in the country. Sometimes she likes it and sometimes she hates it.

Ministers in training

Dexter gets along very well, mostly because she's a quiet person who doesn't like to make waves. Perhaps that's why she's never told anyone in the congregation that she's lesbian, and that when she goes away on her day off, it's to visit her partner.

It's sad, but Dexter may be right about people's reactions. There are urban congregations served by openly gay and lesbian ministers, but Dexter doesn't trust the folks in her congregation enough to come out. Dexter hasn't told anybody, but she's going to look for another church at the end of next year.

That'll come as no surprise to the members. Ministers come and ministers go in this rural church. Some arrive with fire in their eyes to reform the world and rejuvenate the church. Others come in fear and trembling.

Either way, the people of this congregation, more so than in the city churches, know that *they* are the church, not the minister. When all is said and done, they will do it their way, because they were here before the minister and they will be here long afterward.

As for style of worship, they've had everything from fiery evangelical preaching to contemporary poetry. They've sung everything from hot gospel to cool jazz and lukewarm hymnody. Somehow, it all comes out sounding like "Sweet Hour of Prayer."

The people at Oroville United are not cynical. It's just that they've been through about one minister every two years or so, and they find it hard to be impressed with each new one that comes along.

Meanwhile, young Dexter will continue to serve her "apprenticeship" with this congregation. Then they will send her on and wonder who is coming next.

"We do the real training of the ministers here," says Henrietta Crammer, who's been a member of the church for 45 years. "They send them out from the theological schools with all kinds of fancy ideas. We show them what the real church is like."

But always, Henrietta and the others hope that someday a minister will settle down and live with them long enough to learn how decisions really get made in the Oroville-Caustia Pastoral Charge.

Trinity United

Trinity United technically doesn't exist anymore. It had been located in another part of the downtown area. Like First and Central, the demographics changed and they found themselves with just a handful of old and faithful people.

"You didn't have to be very smart to see the writing on the wall," said board chair Frances Robbins. "We had a choice. We could go out with a bang or die with a whimper. And whimpering didn't seem like much fun."

It took a lot of talking, but in the end the decision was unanimous. The church and the property would be sold. The money would be "invested" as gifts to various United Church institutions. Trinity would live on in the imaginative programs made possible by the tiny band of elderly folk who were prepared to invest in a future they themselves would not see.

A few of the Trinity members joined nearby suburban congregations. Sadly, others stopped going to church altogether.

A Colourful Community

I've heard it argued that a denomination should have a definite style, a laid-on worship service, a way of doing things that everybody will recognize right across the country.

That might be more convenient, but it certainly would be less interesting. And less democratic. The United Church has always operated on the idea that the congregation – the local church community – is the primary unit, and that the people there should do things in the way they find most meaningful.

Yes, there are certain rules and procedures to make sure there's fairness and accountability, and we'll get to those in the chapter called "How We Decide." But the local faith community has a lot of freedom to be who they want to be.

In the course of my work, I've visited churches in every corner of this country, and I find the diversity and the creativity delightful. I wouldn't want it any other way.

Finding a church home

My family and I have moved a number of times in our life together, from Canada to the Philippines to Canada to the USA and back to Canada. Each time, we began our orientation into our new community by locating a church, the school, and the public library.

Among other things, the church provided us with the quickest way of getting to know people and developing a new circle of friends. We sensed then, and it's confirmed by more and more science, that physical and emotional health are deeply connected to a sense of living in a community – of having friends you can enjoy and trust.

In 2016, *Time Magazine* published a special edition called *The Science of Happiness*, which over and over pointed to the importance of community. And not just any community.

People who attend church "nearly every week" are, on average, much happier than those who attend "once a month," and even those people are much happier than those who "seldom or never" go to church.

The United Church Observer stated that according to recent research, "regardless of denomination, those who attend worship services more often are happier."

So there you have it. Church is good for you.

It takes work

Friendships, the sense of belonging to a community, isn't something that just happens naturally or by accident. You've got to work at it. Loneliness does more harm to your health than smoking or drugs or chemicals in the environment, or anything else.

Some serious studies have claimed that loneliness has reached epidemic proportions in our hyperconnected electronic culture. Email, Facebook, Skype, Twitter and iPhones don't help one bit. Electronic communication can facilitate some kinds of communication, but it's absolutely no substitute for spending time face to face with a friend. And one of the best ways to find such friends is at church.

But I repeat. It takes work. You need to reach out and take a few risks.

An easy way to start the process of finding a compatible church is to check for a website. Some are using Facebook as their web presence. Not all congregations have them, but websites are becoming increasingly common and necessary. (And, of course, there's the old-fashioned phone book.)

The better websites will tell you a lot about the congregation – its style, its character, and its various programs. The not-so-good ones will at least give you the worship times and a phone number.

But in the end, you need to go there. Not just once, but a number of times and get yourself involved in some of the activities. Don't expect it to happen all on its own.

The mosaic

There are hundreds of varieties of worship in United Churches across Canada. As many varieties as there are congregations. Some of them are very non-traditional.

There is an active French speaking component, *L'Eglise Unie du Canada*, which has taken an earlier edition of this book and translated it into French: *Découvrir l'Eglise Unie*. There are churches using many other languages as well, especially in urban areas where the various tongues of Asia, Africa, the Caribbean, and Latin America are spoken.

Each community finds a way to praise God and to hear the Word in a way that works for them. All of them are struggling to become the community God calls them to be.

Most of them succeed and make a contribution to the rich, colourful mosaic that is The United Church of Canada.

4

All Week Long

So, whether you eat or drink, or whatever you do,
do everything for the glory of God.
1 Corinthians 10:31

What happens on Sunday morning in many congregations is the tip of the iceberg. Some people see it as a celebration of what's been happening all week.

Others, particularly those in the larger congregations, also see Sunday morning as the gathering of the scattered community. A strong church has both: dynamic, rich Sunday morning worship, and small groups where warm support and spiritual growth can be nurtured. One isn't likely to happen without the other.

It's impossible to describe everything that happens in United Churches during the week. Many congregations are really hopping, with things going on practically every night and daytimes, too. Others have very little going on, with Sunday morning being the only important gathering.

It's true, of course that some congregations wouldn't identify with anything that's described in this chapter. They gather on Sunday morning and (especially in rural congregations) it's

a kind of "Sunday dinner" get-together of the church family.

But, I hate to say it, there are some congregations where nothing happens in the middle of the week because nobody does much to make things happen. Which is too bad, because the life of a faith community should extend well beyond what happens in the worship service.

The rewards

There are many lively churches, and they have much to offer us in terms of spiritual, social, and physical health.

The research of social scientists is taking them into all kinds of places they never ventured before, and many of them are finally asking questions about the benefits of being active in a faith community like the church.

It's not about getting into heaven. Yes, Jesus told his friends that their "reward is great in heaven," but he also promised them "life in all its abundance." He was talking about the quality of the life you and I are living right now.

Study after study has found that religious people in all the various faith communities tend to be less depressed and less anxious than nonbelievers, and that this is because of the community, the friendships, and connections that people find in their place of worship.

Simply going to worship on Sunday helps, as do private spiritual practices, but the big benefits just might be in what the church offers Monday through Saturday. That may be what Jesus meant when he said, "Where two or three are gathered in my name, I am there among them."

In many places, there's an increased emphasis on people recognizing that they accompany Christ wherever they are - at school, at work, on a sports team, etc. - and so connect their daily lives with their life in the church.

Congregational events

Congregations often have several big events during the church year when everybody gets together, pitches in, and has a good time. More and more, these events include people of all ages, from tiny tots to the very elderly. Those of us who no longer have children at home really appreciate the youngsters we encounter in church.

Bev and I particularly enjoy the congregational retreat. It's mostly young families with children that go, but it was fun mixing it up with the kids and experiencing the vitality and enthusiasm that surrounded us. We were definitely the "old fogies," but we felt very much at home.

One tradition is the potluck dinner. I've sometimes said that one of the criteria for United Church membership should be a liking for casseroles and jellied salads because that's what you get (mostly) at potlucks. But then I'm told by friends in other denominations that the same thing applies there.

Every congregation, at some time or other, has (or should have) a potluck dinner. Each person brings one dish, whether it's salad or lasagna or raisin pie. These are all laid out on a table and then, as the kids say, "Everybody pigs out"

Somehow, a reasonable balance of courses almost always shows up. I heard of an instance where everybody brought desserts. Wouldn't that be wonderful? The food is always delicious and people have a great time afterwards complaining about having eaten too much. Again.

Potluck dinners are changing because often both partners are working. Many of them make a quick stop at the deli for something to bring.

Usually, there's an event along with the dinner. It may be the annual meeting of the congregation or simply a "fellowship time." Sometimes it's a fundraiser. Whatever the purpose,

eating together is an ancient and honourable way of building bridges of friendship between people.

It also comes very close to the original idea of "Communion." When the people of the early Christian church gathered in the years just after the resurrection of Jesus, they got together for a meal. The tradition of that meal was handed down to us and is celebrated to this day as the Eucharist or Lord's Supper. But there is an element of Holy Communion in every church supper or picnic.

A highlight of the year for me is the annual *Seder* meal on Maundy Thursday just before Easter. This has become a major event for some United Churches.

The Seder is the meal Jewish families eat at Passover, and was the meal Jesus (a faithful Jew) ate with his friends a few days before he was crucified. It is the base on which our communion tradition is founded. Often we move through the various elements of the Seder meal, and sometimes we're lucky enough to have Jewish friends guiding us. The Seder meal then leads us into our Christian communion service.

United Church Women

The most enduring and widespread midweek group is the United Church Women, better known as the UCW. It comes in a variety of styles and sizes.

There's often a deep sense of community among United Church women. They seem to have learned the value of simply being together. Their conversation is not idle gossip, though there may well be some of that. They simply enjoy being together, worshipping together, sharing their lives and their gifts. When they need someone to lean on, they know each other well enough to find friendship and support.

Many United Church Women are worried, however, because

their membership is aging rapidly, and there are not many young women joining. Some are tired of being asked to cater for yet another dinner or funeral. They feel that sort of thing is the responsibility of the whole church – not just the women.

So the UCW is struggling. Many congregations don't have UCWs anymore. But let me quickly add that there are some exciting exceptions to that statement. In many ways, they continue to make a huge contribution to the church. Some congregations rely on the UCW to pay the bills.

There are also women's groups of many kinds that don't call themselves the UCW. (Check out UCW at www.united-church.ca.)

AOTS – As One That Serves

There are groups called United Church Men, or the UCM. Others are called the AOTS. But, let's face it; we guys have never managed to get it together as effectively as the women. And we're poorer for it.

The heyday of the men's movement in the United Church was in the '50s, when almost every congregation had an AOTS group – those letters being taken from the words of Jesus, "I am among you As One That Serves."

Most congregations do not have men's groups. But those that do generally meet once a month, sometimes over dinner, which they bring in from a local fast-food outlet. The main agenda is a chance to talk to each other, to share a few laughs and a few pains, and generally to get to know and support each other.

Here and there, small groups of men are getting together to talk about "men's lib." Some of us are beginning to learn that many things about our male culture put us into cages and keep us from being genuinely free and open to the leading of God.

There's little of what one member called "God talk" at most of the men's meetings. In fact, many men find it hard to talk about their faith or about their feelings. They would be tremendously enriched if they learned how.

I enjoy the men's group at our church. About a dozen of us meet once a month in the morning. There's coffee, but no breakfast. And instead of a "program," what we mostly do is invite men from the group and from outside of it to share their life stories.

In many congregations, there's a kind of informal men's group, which is sometimes the same thing as the Property Committee. They get together to paint the walls or fix the furnace or do any of the hundreds of fix-it things that keep the church building in shape. And there's an amazing amount of fellowship and mutual support that happens in these work parties. (Check out www.aots.ca.)

Non-church groups

There are many different kinds of groups that meet in or around the church. Some simply use the building. There are some struggling towns where the church is the last public building left standing.

There must be hundreds of Alcoholics Anonymous, Al-Anon, and Al-Ateen meetings held in United Churches across the country. There are groups concerned with the handicapped, music, exercise, badminton, dance, and many other activities.

Often ministers refer people to these groups so they can find a bit of friendship and support while they work through their problems.

Many churches now use their Sunday school facilities for nursery school and daycare programs through the week. Often these are run by a committee of parents under the umbrella of

the church organization. In some cases, a private organization rents the facilities.

Some congregations offer space and sometimes leadership to seniors or other groups. And, of course, various community youth groups, such as Cubs, Scouts, Venturers, Brownies, and Guides are often sponsored by congregations.

Our own congregation has a group called Making Connections – a weekly gathering of young mothers and their children. Most of them have no other involvement in the church, though it can be their entry point. These women gather to learn and to share and to support each other. And the children enjoy the playschool.

Church school

The big thing for kids is the Sunday school. Officially, it's called the church school because here and there it meets on a weekday afternoon. Most of the kids and their teachers find it creative, exciting, and really worthwhile.

Of course, there are a few places where Sunday school is just plain dull. Much depends on the attitude of the leaders. If they see it as exciting, and if they're willing to put a bit of work into their preparation, things really happen. The sad news is that in many congregations there are no children.

Many young families become active in the church through the Sunday school. Parents realize their children really miss something if they don't have a religious tradition to give meaning and purpose to life. They realize that keeping a child out of church or Sunday school until they can "make up their own mind," doesn't work. To make a choice, children must have something to choose from – some sense of what such a decision would be about.

A few parents drop their children off at Sunday school with-

out coming to church themselves. That doesn't work either. It sends children a powerful message, a message that says church is really only marginally important. So thinking parents realize that giving children a religious upbringing involves becoming part of the church themselves.

Many churches also offer summer programs, which may be called "Vacation Bible School," or "Vacation Adventure," or something else. These programs often attract children who are not normally a part of the congregation.

No admission fees

There are generally no requirements or prerequisites for children to become part of the Sunday school. Sometimes there's a small registration fee to cover the costs of materials and curriculum but that can usually be waived if necessary.

And I don't think you'll be asked if your child is baptized, or whether you are members of the church or whether you are married. Like the rest of church, there is no dress code for kids in Sunday school. But it can be quite active sometimes, so casual clothes are probably best.

Children are not required to bring an offering, though many parents encourage their children to bring part of their own allowance as an offering. It helps them sense their own participation in the worldwide healing and outreach ministry of the Church.

In most United Churches, Sunday school begins in church, where the children are part of the worship service. Children generally sit with a parent or grandparent for this first part, sometimes joining the minister at the front for the "Word for All Ages," after which they go to their Sunday school sessions.

One of the big problems in all our Sunday schools is that children no longer attend consistently. They come one

Sunday and not the next, sometimes because of other activities they're involved in, sometimes because they alternate between separated parents. That makes it hard for the teachers to create continuity in the program, because every session needs to be a complete learning experience. Which, on the other hand, may also be something positive.

For all the people of God

The adults who work with the children in the church school are not operating in a vacuum. There are lots of helpful, easy-to-use resources.

One of those had its start in Regina a number of years ago, where a group of church school leaders and clergy gathered to look over the materials available at the time.

They were looking for a curriculum that appreciated the gifts children bring to the life of a congregation. They wanted a connection between what adults and children are doing, in worship and in study. None of the existing curricula met their needs. So they swallowed hard and determined to write one themselves.

They approached Wood Lake Publishing, and that embryonic Regina curriculum was developed into *The Whole People of God*. That curriculum is still available online.

The Whole People of God curriculum inspired *Seasons of the Spirit*, which incorporates the same basic principles, but has added a fine art and other components, and includes material that is updated constantly.

A messy church

The "Messy Church" idea is popping up in a lot of congregations. It's a playful concept that takes many different forms. Sometimes it's a 5:30 to 7:30 mid-week, drop-in once a month,

where parents and kids arrive for some fun, a related story of faith, maybe some singing and a nice healthy dinner that other members of the congregation have prepared. It's usually well attended.

Teen groups

Maybe it's wishful thinking, but I have a hunch there's more activity with youth and young adults at United Churches lately. At least, there is in our area. I hear about it a lot from my grandchildren.

It is a very mixed picture, but generally it seems that young people have a higher visibility. They organize themselves under unique names usually invented by the young people themselves. There's a heavy emphasis on social activities. And music. And community service, because many of them genuinely want to make a contribution.

Some are getting involved in the governance of the church and bringing some refreshing young voices into those discussions. My granddaughter, Zoë, quite enjoyed being part of the search committee for a new minister.

Many events are held at a regional level, because individual congregations often do not have enough youth for a group of their own.

Sometimes I'm a bit too optimistic, but my impression is that youth leaders are becoming more creative. However, it seems the youth groups are getting younger. Older teens often leave the church, and there's very little happening in some universities. Happily there are exciting exceptions to that. Some teens become leaders for the younger groups. Many come back to the church when they have children themselves.

The choir

My favourite church group is the choir. Choirs don't get together just to make music for the congregation on Sunday

90

morning. They get together because they enjoy each other and they like to sing.

Most church choirs welcome anyone, even people like me who don't really have a wonderful singing voice. At least, nobody's ever asked me to sing a solo, and there's probably a good reason for that.

Larger churches often have big choirs with professional leaders and even paid soloists and accompanists. Some choirs try to make up with enthusiasm what they don't have in musicianship.

Other congregations have "pick up choirs," where folks commit to creating a choir together one season at a time, such as for Christmas and Easter. Beyond those weeks, they disperse and belt it out from their pew, helping guide the congregation in song from within the crowd.

I know of one church where about a third of the congregation arrives a half-hour ahead of time on Sunday morning and rehearses a song they then sing during the service.

In children's choirs, as with adult choirs, the participating is more important than the performing. Friendships develop, skills are learned, and children begin to appreciate the spiritual and musical heritage we have in the United Church. All this is more important than the quality of the singing.

For me, singing in the choir offers friendship and support, but it is also sometimes the source of some deeply spiritual experiences. Every once in a while, when the choir really gets it together, I have a deep sense of losing myself in the gentle, harmonious embrace of a song and a community.

There's another reason I sing in the choir. Some hard-nosed research tells me that making music, especially singing, is one of the best ways to keep my aging brain from turning into jelly.

Singles and doubles and in-betweens

Many United Churches used to have a couples' club, a singles' or solo club, and various other groups centred around marital status.

Those kinds of groups are still strong and vital in a few places, but, increasingly, people are getting together along lines of interest. There are Bible study groups, as well as groups that look at ecological concerns, gender issues, or social justice problems. Sometimes, very small support groups form around very specific concerns. such a sponsoring refugees.

Many congregations have Amnesty International groups, or groups built around justice issues, or a host of international organizations. Like other congregations, my home church has formed a "sister" relationship with a church in another country. We remember our sister church in El Salvador in prayer every Sunday.

Many ministries

Many churches operate or at least support a food bank, and probably even more have thrift shops. The thrift shops not only recycle clothing, they help people who have limited incomes. Those who work in the shops develop a deep sense of community. They also raise a fair bit of cash, which they offer to various causes or give to support the budget of the church.

Through these groups, we try to make a difference in the world and in our neighbourhood. At the same time, we find a place to belong – a "support group" if you like.

Some groups gather around specific needs. Bev is part of a group that meets to knit prayer shawls, which are given to people when they are ill or facing some other life issues. For a while, our congregation had a group called "Men with wives with cancer." A number of churches have active groups supporting the

"In-from-the-Cold" ministry, which provides a decent and warm place for street people to sleep during the winter.

In my own church, there's a group that gathers after worship called "The Lunch Bunch." Whoever feels like it goes with the group to have lunch at a nearby eatery. Sometimes it's a big group. Sometimes only two or three people go. Many of the people are older singles, who find this an easy and non-threatening way to spend time with other singles.

Bible study groups

Bible study is a long and helpful tradition in the United Church. One reason is because the secular media, while they don't necessarily treat the organized church very kindly, have given a great deal of space to some of the more radical developments in biblical scholarship.

People have begun to realize that the Bible is an exciting book, and that you don't need to be a scholar to study it and learn from its richness. Nor are you required to believe everything that's in the Bible.

When I was first getting involved with the church, I told the minister I didn't believe in a god who zapped people he didn't like and who did all kinds of neat things for people who flattered him.

"I don't believe in that kind of a god either," the minister replied. I soon learned that in the United Church you don't have to believe everything you hear or read. I also learned that God isn't necessarily a "him." God does not have a body like humans, so categories of "he" and "she" don't apply.

Some people are discovering the Bible on the Internet. It's surprising how many different translations and paraphrases of the Bible there are. It's also surprising how much junk there is. And what's really upsetting, how much downright evil there is

in some of the ways God is presented on the Internet. There's also screaming hate from various fundamentalist groups, Christian, Jewish, and Muslim.

In some churches, the preacher meets with a group every week to look at the passages that will be used the coming Sunday. The people in these groups don't tell the preacher what to say, but their study and discussion helps the preacher think through ways in which a given text might be presented, and some of the problems and realities people might bring to the discussion.

A warning! Beware of people who say, "The Bible says..." and then hit you with something that sounds like a commandment from on high. The Bible has been used to justify everything from war to slavery to racism to misogyny to gun ownership.

Bible study is a bit like panning for gold. You may need to slosh a pile of gravel before you begin to find those precious nuggets. But it's worth the effort.

Healing

In the United Church there is a renewed interest in spiritual health. More and more groups are gathering to learn and practise the spiritual art of prayer and healing.

Meditative prayer, spiritual practices, and of course plain and simple, one-to-one conversation with God are finding more vital expression in gatherings that happen at various times – often right before or after church on Sunday.

In my church, as in many others, there's a labyrinth. Some congregations sponsor yoga and Tai Chi classes. There's also Lectio Devina, Enneagram, and various others. We tend to be quite open to new ideas and different ways of exploring our spirituality.

A developing body of research says quite clearly that people who become actively involved in church communities are healthier, happier, and live longer. Their marriages also work out better. (The person who does my income tax also says active church people give more money to all kinds of worthy causes.) Sure, there are a few cranks around. But they are the exception.

And surprise! The medical profession is realizing what faith-filled people have known all along – that everything is connected. Mind, body, and spirit are all one. People who have a spiritual practice and/or are active in a religious community, generally enjoy better health and live longer. In the United Church, we've often tended to concentrate on the mind at the expense of the body and the spirit, but some people tell me that's changing. In many congregations, you will find the language of healing more and more a part of the worship service.

This needs a word of clarification. Don't confuse this spiritual healing with the kind of charade you may have seen some televangelists put on, nor with the sometimes bizarre claims of far out "healers."

There's nothing theatrical in what we do. We are talking about "healing," which is not the same as "curing." When your spirit is healed, your body is more able to fight whatever illness is causing you pain.

A very dear friend mine named Bob Hatfield died some years ago. Bob was a medical doctor. He had struggled for years against leukemia. He used everything that medical science had to offer to overcome his disease, but he worked on his spiritual healing as well, through various forms of meditation, prayer, and humour.

Yes, humour. Laughter can help you heal. Bob lived considerably longer than most of the patients he had himself diag-

nosed with that disease. Was that because of his "laughter therapy" or his spiritual life? There's no way to know. But his strong sense of faith – his spiritual work and his sense of humour – filled his last years with beauty, grace, and meaning.

When Bob and his family finally made the decision to let death proceed, he was able to thank God for all that had been, and to have his loving family around him as he began his final journey into the arms of God. Bob was not cured of his leukemia, but he was healed.

Our congregation, and a number of others, have regular Healing Touch sessions that anyone can make use of, and the phone number of a Healing Touch practitioner is listed every Sunday in the bulletin. Other congregations offer different healing modalities, such as Reiki.

Like a number of congregations, we have a Parish Nurse. She's a volunteer who has a nursing background. She helps us take seriously the concept that Christian healing involves the whole person. The Parish Nurse bridges the gap between theology and medicine, and offers a healing and helpful presence to people of the congregation and community.

She does this individually with members of the congregation who are ill, but she also organizes study sessions where we look at issues such as medically-assisted dying, which has just been legalized in Canada. Some congregations organize blood-pressure clinics, exercise groups, help with visits to the doctor, and a variety of other services and seminars.

A seminar I found particularly useful looked at how we can live creatively and meaningfully during the last years of our lives.

Matchmaking

Not long ago, I had a conversation with a middle-aged woman who talked of "baby hunger." Her children were all grown and although she had grandchildren, they lived on the other side of the continent. She needed children to nurture and to love – children who could sit on her lap.

I told her about the time when our children were young. A woman from our church became their "honorary" Aunt Frances. All our relatives lived far away and the children needed that kind of relationship, as did Frances. She often came to our house just to spend time with the children. She offered practical help and emotional support for our entire family when Bev's mom died a continent away.

In some churches, there's a conscious effort to do some creative "matchmaking." Older persons without children nearby become honorary grandparents to children whose biological grandparents live far away or who are separated by the strains of a divorce.

People going through separation and divorce need emotional support, too, and that can happen if the "matchmaker" puts them in touch with someone who's been through it. New people in the community are partnered with people of similar interests. You can easily think of many other creative matches.

It takes effort, but when the church becomes a caring community that works at meeting the social and spiritual needs of its people, the Holy Spirit has a chance to work and lives are enriched.

Picnics and retreats

The church picnic is another gathering centred around eating. It's often organized by the Sunday school as an end-of-year event and may feature activities that make you realize how old you

really are, such as a three-legged race, tug-o-war, or stilts. Sometimes churches might include a baseball game where middle-aged "athletes" develop sore muscles and sunburns as their kids enjoy out-hitting and out-running them. It may end with a campfire, a singsong, and some prayers.

In some congregations, they have an annual retreat where people of all ages gather for a weekend of fun, study, worship, and just being together. At night there may be a campfire, crazy skits by the kids, lots of songs, and gooey marshmallows.

I remember one of those weekends with particular fondness. As we sat at our lakeside campfire, we were treated to a magnificent lightning storm moving along the other side of the lake. All of us, especially the little ones, sat just a little closer to each other as we experienced God's majesty and the closeness of our community.

Teas and bazaars

Some congregations have an annual tea and/or bazaar, which tend to be big events. Sometimes they are sponsored by the UCW, but one way or another the whole church gets involved, often including the kids.

People bring crafts, cookies, and pies, all of which are spread on long tables and sold for less than reasonable prices. Many churches have an annual rummage sale or garage sale where one person's junk becomes someone else's treasure. Others say it's all about moving stuff from one garage to another.

Used book sales are big. People recycle the books they've read and they buy other books for ridiculously low prices. Garage sales and book sales not only contribute to church finances, they also recycle a whole lot of stuff that might otherwise wind up in the landfill; and the people who come find unbelievable bargains.

These events are quite informal and lots of fun. They attract folks who don't come to the church for any other reason. They're a good excuse to see people you haven't talked to for a while, and a wonderful opportunity to meet some new friends, not to mention gain a few pounds eating too many date squares and cookies. Because I love pies and nobody in our house knows how to make them properly, I fill up the freezer with a year's supply.

In more rural areas, everybody goes to all the teas and bazaars, regardless of whose church is sponsoring them. They become, in effect, community events. And in many places, the United Church is the community church.

Some say the teas and bazaars exist to raise money. Maybe that's because we still can't justify an event just so people can enjoy being with each other. I think we should have such gatherings even if they don't make a dime. They provide some of the cement that holds a community together.

In fact, building community is a major part of the Christian calling.

The wider community of faith

We live in a multicultural society. Canadians, I think, have never really thought in terms of a "melting pot" when considering our rich cultural and religious diversity. "Mosaic" would be a better word.

There are often groups within congregations that reach out and make contact with Buddhists, Muslims, Jews, and other faith groups, and that work to develop understanding with folks from other Christian denominations. There are even United Church congregations with Jewish and Muslim adherents.

Many congregations sponsor and continue to support refugee families, which is not only a fine example of Christian serv-

ice, but also a great experience for those who help the families settle into their new home. Some congregations have gone as far as providing "sanctuary" for those whose legitimate refugee claims may have been denied or processed too slowly.

Community

God, in the biblical tradition, is god of individual persons, yes. But, even more, the God described in the Bible is god of "a people." I really don't think it's possible to be a Christian, or to have any kind of useful spiritual life, without being part of a community. That community needs to worship together. That's central.

But the worship needs to be founded on the caring, growing, studying, working, talking, and playing that's been building the community and binding it together throughout the week.

All of this helps us live happier, heathier, more meaningful lives. And it helps children grow – spiritually, yes, but also physically, socially, and emotionally. It also helps address the epidemic of loneliness that is destroying so many people.

Please don't expect these benefits to come to you after one or two trial visits. When I go swimming in Okanagan Lake near our home, I find it hard to get into the water. Just dipping my toe in, then getting into the water bit by bit prolongs the agony. The alternative is to dive right in, but the shock of the cold water almost gives me heart failure.

But if I tough it out and refuse to retreat to my blanket on the beach, I find the water becomes soothing and comfortable. My swim invigorates and heals and becomes fun.

Getting involved with a faith community is a bit like that. It may not be easy, but if you hang in there, you'll find it healing and invigorating. Being an active member of a faith community is good for you.

5

Hatched, Matched, and Dispatched

While they were eating, Jesus took a loaf of bread,
and after blessing it he broke it, gave it to the disciples,
and said, "Take, eat; this is my body."
Matthew 26:26

Like every other group, church people have their "in" humour. For instance, those people who show up only for baptisms, weddings, and funerals are often called the "hatched, matched, and dispatched" crowd. We don't usually mean it as a put-down. Often, it reflects the pain we feel when people take these events too lightly. Baptisms, weddings, and funerals, plus communion, are very important to us. To understand the church, you need to know why they are so significant.

The sacraments

Some things are almost impossible to explain, and can really only be understood through experience. That's especially true of the concept of sacrament. A sacrament is something we act out because words simply won't hold all the meaning these events have for us.

So how can I possibly describe it? It's a matter of personal experience. Like love. Anyone who has loved another person knows love is real, but they might have a hard time explaining why or how. Poets and songwriters try. Psychologists try. None of them ever completely succeed.

Like love, a sacrament is a mystery. And a mystery can never be explained, but it *can* be experienced. I do hope you'll be open to this experience, and then you'll know why we think they are so important.

There are only two events in the United Church that we call sacraments – baptism and communion. Other denominations see this differently. The Roman Catholic Church, for instance, has seven sacraments.

Sacrament and grace

Maybe a few words will help – though they may sound a bit like jargon. We use that jargon to describe very powerful realities. These words have a very special significance to Christians and I can only do a half-baked job of telling you what they mean. They are words that become fuller and richer as you grow in your faith. Like "love" and "fear," these are emotional words. You don't know what love means until you've been loved. You don't know what fear is until you've been afraid.

So let's give it a try. Two words that have a very significant meaning for Christians: sacrament and grace.

A sacrament is a sacred act, something we do to mark or

point to a holy reality. When I first held my children in my arms, I knew those were sacred moments. When I held the hand of a dying friend, I sensed I was in the presence of something profoundly holy.

Life is full of sacred, holy moments. When we gather together as a church community and together focus our sense of God by reliving a tradition that people have found sacred for many centuries, *that* is a sacrament.

Grace is easier to explain, but harder to understand and accept. Grace is God's love. It's there. All the time. It washes over us. God's love is what keeps the universe going. It's the gas in our tank.

Grace is a gift. And God gives us that gift whether or not we know it or want it or deserve it.

Baptism

Because these concepts mean so much to us, we wince a little when people express some of the outdated ideas that go with sacraments such as baptism. For instance, some believe a baby will "go to hell" if it isn't baptized. Others think a baby doesn't have a name or a soul until that "magic" moment.

I've heard people say that God doesn't love an unbaptized person. Others have said that since a baby was "conceived in sin," and therefore "born bad," it needs to be "washed by baptism" before it's "clean."

Some have wondered whether a child can be baptized when there's only one parent around, or if the baby is adopted or handicapped or if the parents aren't married or if only one of them is a Christian.

Those older ideas no longer work for us. They are part of the outdated, and sometimes really gross popular fiction about the church and what it teaches. Sociologists call those kinds of

ideas "folk religion." They reflect the thinking of people who have an idea that religion somehow protects them from bad things – like a kind of magic – but they never bother to find out what the church is *really* about.

No big deal

For instance, a young couple knocked at our door several years ago. "We were wondering if the Reverend could come over and do our baby. Our folks are here, and we're having a party, so we thought it'd be kinda cute to have the kid done now."

"Well," I said, "Reverend Milton is out right now. She'll be back in an hour. But, I don't think she'd just come over this afternoon and baptize your baby."

"Why not?"

"Because baptism is a big deal. It's something the church takes very seriously. You don't just do it on the spur of the moment. You have to think about the promises you make."

"Promises?" Now they were really confused.

I could see this needed more than a doorstep conversation. "Why don't you phone her, make an appointment, and she can explain what it means to have a child baptized."

They never did. And I suspect they went away feeling the church had somehow turned against them.

Or maybe it was no big deal to them after all.

Nothing but love

The power of what we call "grace" struck me one day in church when the minister was baptizing a baby. Talk about undeserved love! That brand new baby couldn't do much besides fuss and cry, smile a little, eat a lot, and wet her pants.

Her mom and dad beamed down at her with nothing but love in their eyes, and all of us in the congregation smiled and

felt a bit of that love, too.

As the minister made the sign of the cross on the child's forehead, touched her with the oil of healing, kissed her gently, and handed her back to her mom, all of a sudden I knew deep down inside what the minister meant when she talked about "grace."

Inside the parents

When we're talking about the baptism of babies, we're talking, of course, about what happens inside the parents. The baby doesn't know what's going on.

But the parents do. Or they are trying to. We hope the parents and the church community feel the holiness – the sacredness – of this event.

Baptism isn't like one of the shots the baby gets from the public health nurse. It's plain tap water in the baptismal font and it doesn't protect against anything or cause anything. Baptism symbolizes what we hope is happening in the hearts and minds of the parents and of the congregation that has gathered.

If the words and actions don't mean anything to those taking part in the service, they might as well be reciting the alphabet and dancing the rumba for all the good it does. Quite understandably, many ministers and church boards feel it's a bit of a charade if people come to church to say words they don't believe, and participate in a ritual that has no meaning for them.

That's not to say that if you bring a child for baptism you should be able to write a theological paper on the subject. But you should be struggling to understand and to actively live what you believe and you should be willing to try live up to the promises you make in the ceremony. Technically, at least one parent should be a member of the congregation, but it is really up to

the governing body of the church to set the standards and to discuss particular cases.

I was studying in Israel before my first grandchild was born. So I brought back a small bottle of water from the Jordan River for his baptism, and there was enough for his baby sister's baptism a few years later. There's nothing magic about Jordan water. It's the water that comes out of the taps in Jerusalem. It didn't make their baptisms any more or less effective. But for me, it symbolically connected the baptisms of my grandchildren to the powerful story of Jesus and the moment of his baptism.

I was doubly delighted when Bev developed a book paralleling our grandchildren's baptisms with the baptism of Jesus. It included pictures of the children and, of course, pictures of Jesus. It's a book you can customize for the children in your life. It's called *My Baptism*. If you buy that book, take a look at the beautiful child on the cover. That's my granddaughter, Zoë! (Available at www.woodlakebooks.com.)

The promises

So what are those promises we make at a baptism? First, the parent or parents are asked whether they really want this child to be a member of the Christian church. Baptism isn't about joining The United Church of Canada. It's a welcome into the *whole* church of God. All over the world. All the denominations. The word on the baptism certificate is "catholic" – the baptism is into the catholic (i.e., *universal*) church.

Not all denominations agree, but that's how we see it in the United Church. And, of course, that means that if you've been baptized in another Christian church, the United Church recognizes your baptism.

Next, the parent(s) are asked whether they believe in God.

If they don't, the rest of the questions, in fact the whole thing, would be pointless. They are asked whether they'll provide a Christian home for the child and whether they'll encourage the child to be part of the church. They are also asked if they "will join with your brothers and sisters in the mission and ministry of Christ's church."

If the parent(s) say "yes" to that, then the congregation also has some promises to make. In our tradition, the whole congregation becomes the sponsor or "godparents" of the child, which is why we're not very enthusiastic about private baptisms in the home. It's the congregation's responsibility to help the parents and the child experience the love of God. That's also why we prefer baptisms to happen in the child and parents' home congregation.

So the congregation is asked to say "yes," they want that child as part of their community, and they accept their share of the responsibility for that child's growing up.

When all those commitments are made, the baptism is performed. At least that's the usual order. I know of one minister who performed the baptism first, before the promises, because he felt God's grace was there for the child regardless of what the parents or the congregation said or did.

There are, of course, special cases and special circumstances. Talk them over with your minister.

Family enrichment

When Bev and I had our kids baptized, we promised to raise them in the church family. It meant being involved with the church ourselves. It also meant a conscious effort to teach them what it means to be Christian, which is about far more than saying grace at meals, going to church once in a while, and being nice to each other.

Bev wasn't an ordained minister when we first made those promises with our children. We were just like every other family, trying to figure out how to make sense out of life. Looking back, we realize the commitments we made really enriched our whole family. We and our children have gained far more than we've given.

It seemed to us that we couldn't live up to the promises we made when our children were baptized unless we got involved with the church. It's like being sure your kids are educated. First, you need a school. Sure, there are some who manage to educate their children at home, but they are few and far between. There are also a few parents who have given their children a complete religious education at home, but they're exceptions.

Not that Christianity is strictly a church affair, any more than education only happens in school. We teach our kids far more at home than the school or the church ever could. But school and church are still important. I'd say they are essential.

Who decides?

More and more United Church leaders are taking a tougher stand on the baptism of infants. Parents who have had one baby baptized but who haven't darkened the door of the church since might be asked a few more questions when they come around with baby number two. "You didn't live up to your promises the first time. How can we help you live up to them this time?"

That's why few clergy will baptize children unless at least one parent takes part in a preparation program. Sure, that means some people go off in a snit. It also means that those who take it seriously enough to do some preparation are much more likely to live out their promises.

Policies

Congregational policies on baptism vary. In some churches, any parent who wants a child baptized gets a child baptized. Others require parents to sign a statement of faith and a promise of church participation.

Most congregational policies simply say that the parents should understand what it is they are doing and promising. The parents should really know what these statements and promises mean, now and in the future. If the church board is satisfied that the parents understand, then it's usually up to those parents and their own conscience to decide what should be done.

Unfortunately, church boards often don't take their responsibility seriously. They heap it all on the minister. In the United Church, it's the governing body's responsibility to decide who gets baptized. If they take that responsibility lightly, it's no wonder so many parents think of it simply as "a cute thing to do."

The baptismal ceremony

In the United Church, baptism takes place during a regular worship service. Often, an elder or a member of the church's governing body introduces the family and the child to the congregation. Then, after the parent or parents have been asked to make some promises about the child's upbringing, the minister takes the child from the parent and with water makes the sign of the cross on the baby's forehead.

Some ministers will just sprinkle a bit of water on the child's head; others use the water more liberally. This may be followed by a touch of oil (don't worry – it's ordinary olive oil) to the baby's forehead as a symbol of healing and peace.

The words spoken at this time are usually, "I baptize you in

the name of the Father and of the Son and of the Holy Spirit" – words that are used in almost all churches in the worldwide community. That is followed by a blessing. The minister tells us that the child has been welcomed into the community of faith. Then the child is handed back to the parent. Often a baptismal candle, a children's Bible, and a certificate are given.

Of course, some children refuse to be held by any stranger, minister or not. If that happens, the parent simply holds the child while the baptism is performed. Older children stand beside a parent for their baptism.

Don't be upset if your baby cries. He or she will not be the first or the last child to find the process a little strange. Perhaps even frightening.

I like Jesus

I remember one memorable service when Bev baptized three children from one family. The youngest child was about five. Bev had spent time not only with the parents but with the children, helping them understand what baptism was about. She used a puppet to show them what was going to happen.

At the service, the two older children read very simple statements about what baptism meant: "I like Jesus," said one. "Church people are nice," said the other. Not heavy-duty theology, but their own words. The smallest boy held up a picture he had created.

Often, when the child being baptized has older sisters or brothers, those other children join their parents around the baptismal font and, as far as they can understand, share in the vows their parents are making. It's also a good occasion for the parents to explain to the older children and to friends what baptism means, and to recall the day when they were baptized.

Sometimes one parent wants a child baptized and the other

doesn't. That situation should be discussed with the minister. In most instances, if one parent can't, in good conscience, make the vows, that decision should be respected. But that parent should at least agree to the other parent taking those vows, including the part about raising the child in the Christian faith. Otherwise, baptism may simply drive a wedge between the parents.

Wood Lake Publishing and other publishers offer resources that help enrich and explain the theology and the symbolism of baptism. Don't hesitate to check them out if you have more questions.

Adult baptism

Infant baptism is the most common practice in the United Church, but adults also sometimes decide to be baptized. Parents have the right to decide against infant baptism and to wait for the kids to make the faith commitment for themselves.

I was baptized as an adult, after I was married. It was a deeply moving experience for me, one in which I felt very close to God. I was raised in the Mennonite tradition, which teaches that people should only be baptized when they are adults and can understand what they are promising.

I made essentially the same promises at my own baptism as I made at my son's a few months later. I declared myself a Christian and promised to try with all my heart to be faithful to what that meant. I promised to receive the nurture and support of the Christian community, to try to grow in my understanding of my faith, and to work for God's justice and love in this world.

When I think about it, that was really a dedication of my whole life.

Membership

A different attitude about "membership" seems to be growing in the United Church. On the one hand, there are many people who hardly ever darken the church door who consider themselves to be "United Church." They expect the church will be there when they need it for a wedding or serious illness or a funeral, but they don't support it, financially or in person.

Perhaps they think it's like some countries in Europe where the church is supported by taxes. But in Canada, it's the hard work and the cash of those who actively support the church that keep it alive. And it's understandable when these active supporters get a bit ticked off at people who want the church to be there when they need it, but they never support it.

On the other hand, there are increasing numbers of people who are very active in the United Church, but who never join officially. They may have come from another denomination and simply don't want to cut those ties.

Others come from no denomination at all. They simply don't see the importance of formal membership and, for that matter, neither do most others in the congregation. Many people think that if you show up with some regularity and support the church in some way, you are a member.

This can get dicey on occasion because, technically, only members can vote on those things that relate to the faith of a congregation. That rule is often blissfully ignored, but there may be times (such as voting on whether to call a new minister) when a presbytery representative or someone else may insist that only members can vote.

Or at least, that is the way things stand now. The whole issue of what constitutes membership in the United Church is being reviewed, and some changes may well have been made by the time you read this book. So ask your minister to bring you up to date.

Confirmation

In the traditional United Church pattern, children are baptized as infants and go to Sunday school until they reach their early teens. At that point, they take a class, usually taught by the minister, which runs anywhere from a few weeks to a year. At the end of that time, the young person is expected to decide whether or not to confirm what their parents declared on their behalf a dozen years earlier.

We used to call that "joining the church," but now a child joins the church at baptism. The traditional word is "confirmation," when the child confirms the promises made by its parents.

When children get to be adults, they often realize how much they don't know. For them, and for others of various ages coming into the church for many reasons, congregations often have a series of study sessions each year to look at what it means to be part of the church.

Since the early 1980s, many people in those study sessions have been using this book (this is the fourth edition) as an introductory text to The United Church of Canada. I wrote the first edition of this book back in the early 1980s because a minister said to me, "I have ten fine, capable people on my board. But none of them have any background in the church, United or otherwise."

So this book has been a bestseller (exceeded only by hymn books and Bibles) in United Church bookstores through three editions. We'll see what happens with this one.

Children and communion

Until the late 1980s, teenagers took their first communion after they were confirmed. That's still the situation in some congregations. The idea is that people don't take communion

until they are able to make their own profession of faith.

However, in many congregations, children may take communion if that is the parents' choice. This isn't true in all areas of the country, but the practice is spreading.

The problem with communion in the United Church is not the technicalities of who can and who can't receive it. The celebration of communion is probably the most important act of worship we have in our denomination (as in most other denominations) and we don't take it seriously enough.

Passover

What we call communion is often called the Mass in some denominations, although the word "Mass" actually refers to the whole service. Eucharist is another term that's often used, as is the "Lord's Supper" and the "Last Supper."

Like baptism, communion is a sacrament that goes back to Bible times. Jesus participated in both. The Bible tells us the story of how he was baptized in the Jordan River.

The first Lord's Supper was part of an even older tradition, the Passover meal. As a faithful Jew, Jesus celebrated the Passover every year.

The Passover recalls the time, centuries before Jesus, when the people of Israel were held as slaves in Egypt, and Moses led them out of captivity into the "Promised Land."

That experience became the central metaphor for the Hebrew people – the knowledge that God had delivered them out of slavery and into freedom. That's why the Passover feast is the most important event in the Jewish calendar.

The Passover feast was a full meal. The one Jesus ate with his disciples just before he was executed – the meal we usually call the "Lord's Supper" – probably included a leg of lamb, bread, and wine.

The Bible writers tell us that during that meal, Jesus took the bread, thanked God for it, broke it, and passed it around. He said the bread symbolized his body, "broken for you."

Then he took the wine, which he described as "my blood, shed for you," and asked his disciples to think of that as a symbol of a new kind of relationship with God. He called it "the new covenant."

The covenant

Covenant is a word we don't use too much outside of the church. Lawyers sometimes use it to mean an agreement. In church, it means that and a whole lot more.

When our children became part of our family, through birth and through adoption, Bev and I made a one-way covenant with them, even though we didn't put it into any words. We knew we would love our kids, come hell or high water.

Bev and I haven't always been ideal parents, and our kids haven't always loved us back. In other words, we've been a normal family. But the covenant is there because we can never stop being their mom and dad, no matter what we may do to them. Or what they might do to us.

God's covenant begins as a one-way promise. Over and over again in the Bible, God says in a variety of ways, "I love you. I promise that I always will. Whether you love me back or not."

We can respond to that love and make it a two-way covenant. That's what we do in the sacraments of baptism and communion.

Communion

When we symbolically reenact that meal in the ritual we call "communion," we are saying "yes" to that special covenant relationship God has with the people of the Word, the church.

Sharing the Lord's Supper with our fellow Christians is what we call "a means of grace." Grace is that special, undeserved love that God lavishes on us. Communion is one of the ways we can stay in touch with that love.

It's not that the bread and the wine (often called the "elements") are anything special. In fact, it's usually ordinary bread from the local grocery, though I think communion is nicer when the bread is homemade. Sometimes it's also gluten free, so that everyone can take part in the service. As for the wine, it is probably not wine at all, but grape juice.

That's all part of the symbolism. God can take plain ordinary bread and grape juice and give them a meaning that'll shake us to our roots. In the same way, God can take plain ordinary people, shake us to our roots, and make us part of God's dream for a hurting world.

Whether any of that happens or not depends on what we bring to communion. The circumstances under which the Last Supper is celebrated, the music and the surroundings, may help.

But the essential thing is our faith.

The communion service

There are many ways of celebrating the Lord's Supper. Often congregations use different rituals at different times. And being who we are in the United Church, there are lots of variations on the descriptions that follow.

The traditional United Church way of serving communion is for some elders to come forward. The minister gives them trays with the bread, which has been cut into cubes, and a chalice of grape juice or wine. Some churches use tiny glasses.

The minister and those assisting are on one side of the communion table and the congregation on the other. That arrangement is an important symbol. We gather around the

Lord's table, as a covenant community, and eat together.

Traditionally, elders (or board members) serve us, and we serve each other, passing the bread and the cup to the person sitting beside us. In many congregations, any active member may be asked to be a server, including children.

Serving one another symbolizes our caring ministry to each other. When someone serves me the bread and wine during the communion in church, that person is offering me a symbol of God's most precious gift to us – divine love, which we call grace.

Another common practice is for the minister and an elder to stand at the front of the church. The elder (or sometimes another minister) holds a loaf of bread and the minister holds the chalice.

People come up to the front of the church. Each person breaks off some bread, dips it in the wine, and "partakes" right there. Sometimes, usually with smaller groups, the chalice and the loaf may be passed or taken around.

An important part of the symbolism in communion is that Jesus is the host at this meal and we are all his very welcome guests.

An informal affair

Some congregations that treasure a strong Methodist heritage, such as the churches in Newfoundland, ask members to come up to the communion rail that runs across the front (chancel) of the church, where they are served communion.

In the United Church tradition, only ordained clergy or specially licensed members can preside at communion. However, in small study or fellowship groups, people may have something called an "*agape* meal" or "love feast," without a minister present.

Usually, an *agape* meal is a very informal affair, where food

and drink (it may be bread and wine, or something else) are passed around as a symbol of the love and affection in that group. This can be very beautiful and meaningful, but, officially at least, it's not communion.

Sometimes in a restaurant, instead of saying grace, someone may take a piece of bread, break off pieces and give them to the others around the table. It's not communion, but it's a beautiful symbol of our shared faith.

Generally, in most United Churches, communion is celebrated once a month, but in some cases more frequently. Some congregations only celebrate communion four times a year.

Open communion

The United Church practises "open communion." That means we welcome the members of every other denomination, and well as those who don't belong to any church.

There are people who feel you can only come to communion if you are "living a good Christian life," but in the United Church we come out of our need. I can come to God's table no matter how badly I've messed up my life. In fact, that's when I most need to receive communion.

In other words, communion is not just for those who have their lives all together. If that were the case, none of us, including the clergy, would qualify. It's not a matter of *deserving* communion. It's a gift. Communion is a symbol of God's love for us, God's grace, especially when we are writhing around in our own muck.

And the communion table is God's table, where everyone is welcome!

Everyone!

Here comes the groom

Marriage is considered a sacrament in some denominations, but not in the United Church. Our attitude toward weddings is criticized by some as being too "easy-going," and praised by others as being "open-minded."

Until recently, you couldn't get a decent civil wedding in many parts of Canada. If you went to the Justice of the Peace, "JP," you got ten minutes in a stuffy room on a weekday. People who wanted a ceremony to give the moment some significance, and a few friends and relatives to stand with them, had to go to the church whether they believed in God or not.

Fortunately, those days are gone. There are marriage commissioners who often do very fine wedding services. Now, most people who come to the church to be married do so because they genuinely want a church wedding, although there are still a few who don't know that alternatives exist.

Often people want a Christian wedding, but not in the church building. Many clergy are okay with that. The last few weddings I've attended were in a park or a garden. That's becoming increasingly common.

Sometimes couples want a church wedding for purely sentimental reasons. "My mother was married in a church and she thinks I should be married in one, too." Or, "It's such a pretty place with a nice centre aisle and we did want a traditional wedding. Besides, the minister is so good-looking."

That kind of thinking raises questions of integrity. When people are married by a Christian minister, it is a religious service – a service of worship whether it is in a church building or not. A wedding is the celebration of a covenant – a special, committed relationship – before God and before God's people. It's something the minister might want to discuss with the couple so that people aren't repeating vows that have no meaning for them.

This is not to say that a couple with differing religious traditions should not be married in a church. United Church clergy are usually open and sensitive to the faith of others, whether the person is from another Christian denomination or from another faith tradition.

United Church clergy are often very happy to have clergy or leaders from other religious groups participate in the service. Likewise, I have known many United Church ministers who have participated in weddings held in other churches, temples, synagogues, and mosques.

There are also occasions when only one of the couple has a faith that brings them into the church for marriage. This should be thoroughly discussed with the minister, and the non-Christian partner should understand what is going on and agree to it, but should not be asked to say things he or she doesn't believe.

Same gender couples

Gay and lesbian couples are now coming forward to be married in the church or, if not in a church building per se, then with a Christian ceremony. Congregations that have made a commitment to be an "Affirming" church will do this, as will many others. But the minister and the governing body of the church can refuse, if their conscience forbids it, provided they give the couple the name of a nearby United Church that would be willing to do the service.

Marriage preparation

More and more United Church congregations insist that the couple have some preparation for marriage or covenanting. Clergy feel that if they are going to "tie the knot," they would like to do what they can to see that it holds.

In some large cities, couples may be asked to go to interde-nominational marriage preparation courses. Some congrega-tions simply schedule marriage preparation events at regular intervals, and work with several couples at the same time. In smaller churches, the minister is more likely to have two or three private sessions with the couple.

The counselling doesn't lay a "religious trip" on the cou-ple, at least not as a rule. It's intended to help them face some of the questions that are bound to give them trouble if they don't deal with them creatively. It's amazing how many seri-ous questions about sex, children, relatives, work sharing, money, and other things many couples never discuss prior to getting married.

Most couples coming to be married are already living to-gether. "We've already worked out all the problems," they say. "We know we can make it." But it doesn't work out that way. Something about being officially married changes the relation-ship fundamentally.

Even people who are on their second or third marriage need preparation. Often, they don't really understand what went wrong the first or even the second time around.

Even people who have been together for years need to work on their relationship. Marriage is like a garden. It needs water-ing, fertilizing, and weeding. If you don't keep working at it, you wind up with an unproductive tangle of emotional weeds. And there are times in every relationship when outside, profes-sional help is needed.

Bev and I would not be together, thoroughly enjoying our love and friendship after 60 years together, if we had not strug-gled through some very tough times with the help of a profes-sional counsellor.

The arrangements

Weddings are almost always held on Saturday. I suppose this is because it's the only day of the week when wedding guests aren't working and the church is available. I don't know many clergy who will do a wedding on a Sunday, although I know of one instance where a couple, who had been very involved with the congregation, were married as part of the regular Sunday worship.

If you want to make clergy livid, arrange for the reception hall and everything else and then call the minister at the last moment. It's a great way to get off on the wrong foot. Ministers usually have very busy schedules and need lots of advance warning to arrange marriage preparation and wedding times.

Always phone the church first. Ask about the process. Or check out the congregational website. In some congregations, couples are asked to fill out a form and agree to certain things before they even begin to discuss a date. It's not as automatic as some people think it is.

Enthusiastic friends and relatives sometimes cause problems at weddings. People popping up and down to take photos with their iPhone hardly add to the dignity of what is, after all, a service of worship, when all of us yearn to understand the mystery at the heart of love.

Most often, wedding guests are allowed to take as many photos as they want while the wedding party is assembling. Then they are told "no photos please" until the signing of the register. Some liberties may be granted to a "designated photographer," who has discussed the protocol with the minister before the wedding.

Videotaping enthusiasts can easily turn a sacred service into a silly circus. Having spent years as a professional TV producer, I can tell you there is no need for the camera person to be pop-

ping up and down, shooting from all kinds of angles and using additional lighting.

Competent, sensitive videographers will set up their camera on a tripod in some inconspicuous place, usually at the back or the side of the church and stay there relying on a long lens to get the shot. If they don't own a long lens, they rent one.

Payment

When Bev and I were married, we slipped the minister a ten-spot in a white envelope and thought that covered things. Looking back, I know it didn't, even then.

Bev was a member of that church, but up until that point I had made no contribution to that or any other church. Nowadays, many United Churches have a fee schedule that includes something for the use of the church, the caretaker, the organist, and the minister's time. Ask about these charges when you phone the church office.

If, as is most often the case now, it's only the minister who is involved in a wedding that takes place outside the church building, then it's a matter of discovering what his/her expectations are.

"Wedding planners" are a new breed of service providers. Some are very helpful and useful. Others act as if the minister is a sub-contractor. That does not help.

Ask. Don't make assumptions.

Who can and who can't

There are no hard and fast rules in the United Church about who can get married in the church and who can't. It's up to the church board to make that decision. Often, divorced people come because they feel they have been rejected by their own denomination. They want to get married again, but their own

THIS UNITED CHURCH OF OURS

church won't do it. Many clergy feel they have a ministry to these people, to help them when they are trying to put their lives back together.

Very young people or couples coming to get married only because the bride is pregnant may run into some tough questions from clergy. Clergy have the right to refuse to perform a wedding when they feel it would be wrong.

As far as I know, only the United Churches, the Unitarian Universalist Church, Metropolitan Community Churches, and the Anglican Church of Canada will do weddings for lesbian and gay couples.

Variations and gimmicks

For a while, the "in" thing was for couples to write their own wedding ceremony, complete with poems by Kahlil Gibran and a friend with a guitar singing "The Wedding Song."

I have the impression that weddings have become much more traditional lately and that couples are choosing the "standard" service. We haven't gone all the way back to quavering tenors singing "My Hero" and a nervous groom trying to say, "and thereto I plight thee my troth," but few couples today want to write their own ceremony.

Instead, most clergy offer a choice of two or three services and the couple can choose among them. Whether alterations to the wording are allowed depends on the minister.

Another fad that (thankfully) seems to be passing is having the wedding in wild and wonderful circumstances – on mountaintops or floating through the air in parachutes. Bev has turned down requests to do weddings on horseback and in a floating disco. Few clergy have much patience with that sort of thing and some refuse to do weddings outside the church building.

Still, I do know one United Church minister who did a wedding in a Concorde jet. I don't know if it was before or after it broke the sound barrier.

Funerals

If weddings are a complication for United Church clergy, funerals are even more so. There are a variety of names for the service that happens when someone dies: memorial service, celebration of life, service of remembrance. Sometimes those names communicate subtle differences of meaning, so it's wise to ask for clarification if you are not sure what is being offered or suggested.

Of course, when pople plan for weddings, there's time to talk about what is going to happen and what it means, but when people find themselves making funeral arrangements for a loved one, there's seldom much notice and perhaps little opportunity to discuss what these arrangements mean and what the options are. That's why the church has always encouraged people to discuss, with their loved ones, their own preferences regarding funeral arrangements, while they are still hale and hearty.

It's good to remember that a funeral service, like a wedding or a baptism, is a service of worship. It's sad and upsetting when it turns into a kind of circus with a succession of people coming up to tell funny stories about the deceased. That's a personal opinion, of course.

For many people, the sharing of personal stories, humorous or otherwise, can be the most healing and significant part of the service. These are stories that personalize the service. I've been to services where the deceased was barely mentioned.

Most clergy will want to meet with the family to talk about the kind of service that would be a most appropriate way to

celebrate and remember the life of the one who has died.

Please contact the church as soon as possible. Good communication can prevent a lot of hassles and disappointments. Clergy are busy people and churches are busy places, as are funeral homes.

I will always remember my anger at my father's funeral. At her most vulnerable moment, the funeral director talked Mom into an elaborate and expensive service that my dad would have hated. And Mom hated it, too. Furthermore, she couldn't afford it.

Many congregations run educational events to discuss death and dying. There's much to be said and learned about representation agreements, wills, funeral homes and funerals, and other matters that seem to come up suddenly and unexpectedly when a loved one dies. I've found such events really helpful. Preparation can soften a lot of pain.

Among other things, it has helped Bev and me to have serious, candid discussions with our children and grandchildren. Those conversations have been good and have strengthened our family ties.

When a loved one dies, there is grief. There is sadness. That's normal and good. But it can become a painful and negative experience if the decisions that need to be made at this time turn into a series of hassles.

While you're thinking about death, be sure to make a will. That way, whatever you leave when you die won't all get used up for lawyers' fees, or go to the government. And think about the church when you are making your will. Many people leave money to the church because they want to continue to contribute to God's work, even after they are gone.

The gift of life

Possibly more important than all of that is a conversation with your loved ones about the meaning of life and the process of dying. All of us will die, and none of us know when or under what circumstances.

For myself, I don't want to be kept alive by heroic means when there's no longer a reasonable possibility of recovering. I would like my family and my doctor to gently "pull the plug" if that time comes. Also, if there are any used parts still good to anyone, in medical research for instance, they're welcome. The legalities around that are different in each province, so ask your doctor what you need to do to make that possible.

I would also like the option of saying to my family and my doctor, "This pain, this illness, has become intolerable. My life is over. Please help me end it." That's a very personal feeling, of course.

Because assisted dying has now become a legal possibility in Canada, it's really important to talk about that with family and loved ones while you are still healthy, so those terribly difficult decisions are not all dropped on them in the midst of their grief. Planning ahead allows the family to know your wishes, which can help them avoid unnecessary tension or outright conflict after you are gone.

There's nothing "morbid" or "sick" about discussing your own death. Talking about it won't make it come any faster or delay it any longer. You are simply acknowledging a fact. Life is terminal.

Hospice care is now available in many places. Hospices are generally run by caring, sensitive professionals and volunteers who can make the last days or weeks of a person's life a genuine blessing to all concerned. Be sure to let your church know so that spiritual care can also be provided.

The service

If the one who died was an active church person, then funeral or memorial services might be held in the church, in spite of what some funeral directors may tell you. It's a proper place to say goodbye and to thank God for the life that has been lived.

Although these things vary from region to region and from church to church, it's generally not a United Church tradition to have an open casket, at least not in church during the service. In some instances, the coffin, if there is one, may be open during a wake or at the funeral home.

But again, this is one of those things that varies so much between families and cultures. Talk about it with the minister when you are arranging the service.

More and more people, for some very good reasons, are choosing cremation. Bev and I have told our family that's what we would like. When the body has been cremated and the casket is not present, the service of worship is called a "memorial service," or a "celebration of life." If the service is held in a church, the funeral director does not need be involved in that part of it at all.

You still need a funeral director, however, because they are in the best position to handle cremation and many of the legal and other matters relating to a death.

Bev and I have joined a memorial society, which ensures that when we die our funeral expenses will be kept to a minimum. Funeral costs can be far higher than you might expect, as they were in the case of my father's funeral.

For the mourners

A memorial service or a funeral should give us an opportunity to acknowledge our grief and our pain. It's a time when we shed our tears openly and we ask God to be with us in our sorrow.

But it should also be a service of thanksgiving. We need to thank God for the life that was lived and then to say goodbye to a friend or loved one.

It's easy to forget about the children. They also have a need to say goodbye – to mourn for someone they cared about. I don't think they should be shielded from the grief that surrounds a death, and they certainly shouldn't be told little white lies to make the pain easier. Let the children grieve, too.

Bev and I attended a wonderful memorial service for a woman who had been very active in working with children in her church. Not only were there several dozen children present at the service, but one of the ministers took the time to sit down with the children to tell them what had happened to their friend, and to give them a special message which their friend had sent just before she died.

Sharing the pain

I'm always a bit upset when there is no service of any kind to celebrate the life of someone I cared about. I see it often in the newspapers: "No service, at the request of the deceased."

The funeral or memorial service isn't for the person who died. It is for those of us who are left behind. We need a way, for both psychological and faith reasons, to to get together to share our sadness and to do the kind of grief work that all human beings must do at such times.

Christmas can be a very difficult time for people who have recently lost someone close to them, and for those who are dreading another Christmas alone. Because of this, many congregations have a special service a week or so before Christmas. Some call it "Blue Christmas," while others call it, "The Longest Night," and some simply call it a "Service of Remembering." This service provides a way to express some of the grief we feel, and anger too sometimes, during a season when most of

the world, and especially the media, is promoting joy, happiness, and family warmth.

The year Bev and I lost our son Lloyd, we found the Blue Christmas service deeply moving and helpful. We go every year to remember his life, and often the lives of friends we've lost during the year.

And we go to stand beside others who carry their pain into the Christmas season.

Celebrating the pilgrimage

There are other events in the journey from birth through death that can and should be celebrated in church. Some congregations have ceremonies to celebrate a youngster moving from childhood to adulthood, usually on the 12th or 13th birthday. This is a gift from the Jewish tradition, where it is called a *bar* or *bat mitzvah*.

Some churches take part of a Sunday morning worship service to honour those who have graduated from high school or university.

Bev and I had a service of rededication on our 25th wedding anniversary. Some congregations have an annual rededication service near February 14th, Valentine's Day. Occasionally, people even come to mourn the death of a marriage when they face divorce.

The word "celebrate" has a unique meaning in the church. We mean much more than a party. It means to mark an occasion, to make it memorable, and most of all, to see the hand of God in it.

So we "celebrate" birth and death, coming together and going away. Our whole lives are wrapped in the love of a caring community, and in the arms of a loving God.

6

Telling the New-Old Story

*"The Spirit of the Lord is upon me, because the Most High
has anointed me to bring good news to the poor.
God has sent me to proclaim release to the captives and
recovery of sight to the blind, to let the oppressed go free, and
to proclaim the year of God's favour."*
Luke 4:18–19(NRSV, adapted)

S tuart Daly was one of the busiest doctors in the small city of Trail, British Columbia. I have no idea whether he was the best doctor or whether he saw more patients. But I am willing to bet he spent more time with each patient than almost any other medic.

Dr. Daly cared very deeply about people, even those he had never met before. I'd heard about him, so when Bev and I had

the flu, we called him. Dr. Daly loved house calls.

After a couple of needles in our backsides, he sat on the edge of the bed and talked for half an hour.

That wasn't unusual, we soon found out. We heard from others that after bringing news of a loved-one's death, he might stay for hours, sometimes all night, to help the person through those first hours of pain and grief.

Dr. Daly would never force his faith on anyone. If you asked him a question, you got a straight answer. Otherwise, his faith was expressed more by his actions than by his words.

And he certainly wasn't short of words. Dr. Daly was very articulate about his faith and he enjoyed talking about it. But he felt the life you led communicated far more than the words you spoke, and unless your faith made a big difference to every part of your living, the words were empty.

He wasn't saying you go around doing nice things, hoping somebody will notice and be sufficiently impressed so they'll hold still while you bend their ear. Dr. Daly helped people because he liked them and cared about them, whether they ever knew he was a Christian or not.

When I think of what the United Church means by words like "mission," "evangelism," and "ministry," I always think of Dr. Stuart Daly.

Evangelistic styles

When we were living in the Philippines, we got to know missionaries from other denominations. One couple, from a small faith group, seemed to live particularly well. They had a lovely house, a big car, and a warehouse full of rich food imported from the U.S. These people spent at least three-quarters of their time writing letters home to raise money for their "work" in the Philippines.

Not far away, another missionary couple lived very poorly. They didn't really have enough and what they did have they kept giving away. They didn't have much time to write those money-raising letters because they were too busy helping people.

Those two styles of mission are evident here in Canada as well. We can see them on a larger scale in the way different organizations and groups reach out to others.

Some religious organizations do a very clever job of selling. They use the same sales techniques as other kinds of advertisers, spending millions to run TV specials. They develop extensive mailing lists and send out glossy brochures and have sophisticated social media campaigns. The cost in money and personnel is fantastic.

At the local level, there's a high proportion of time and energy spent in telling themselves what wonderful things they are accomplishing and that they are doing all these things because they are Christian.

The United Church seems to be at the other end of the spectrum. As individuals, you hardly ever hear a peep out of us concerning our faith. We're often too timid to point to the hand of God active in life around us. We're often too embarrassed to raise the subject of faith, so we miss many opportunities to share the good news. United Church people are not good at talking about the things that make them tick.

Thankfully, there are signs that this is beginning to change. There have been events at which people have shared their faith from a wide range of experiences. I hope that trend continues and grows.

While we're still not good at talking about our faith, we're reasonably good at *doing* the WORD, of *living* our faith. The United Church record of working with people nobody else cares

about, or going to bat for the underdog, is certainly better than most.

For instance, it's no accident that so many food banks and thrift shops are located in, or supported by, United Churches. It's no accident that United Church people were at the forefront of the various freedom movements, from women's liberation to racial justice and the acceptance of the LGBTQ community.

Doing and telling

I wish we could learn to tell our stories – to talk openly about what we believe and why we believe it. There are some in the United Church who insist it's best to simply work for God's *shalom* (peace), to do God's will, and to struggle for truth and justice. Sooner or later people will realize why we are doing these things and will start to ask questions.

It's a good theory, but I don't think it works. I'm not suggesting that we start bragging about what we do, but I think we need to talk about what we believe and why. Not with overblown theological discourse, but with simple, personal stories. We can do that with honesty, integrity, and good taste. How can our church grow (or even survive) unless we can tell others what puts the bounce in our step?

Jesus challenged us not to "hide your light." Our faith stories can be told with gentleness and integrity. We can talk about what we do and why we do it without backing people into a corner or insulting their intelligence. It takes a bit more skill, but it can and should be done.

One to one

It's true. Some people have sold religion like an underarm deodorant designed to make you acceptable and popular. A genu-

ine faith is not communicated that way.

The oldest and still the best way to communicate our faith is also the simplest. We talk about our faith the same way and in the same places we talk about everything else. The "front lines" of faith are at home over dinner, driving in the car, over coffee at work, in the aisle at the supermarket, or on the golf course.

There's absolutely nothing more important than telling the story of faith in these everyday places. That's how the gospel spread in the first place and that will always be its most effective communication. No church service, no rally, no television program, no book, no plan or program is as important as this. Yet, in the United Church, that's the kind of communicating we do least well.

Sometimes we use the clergy as a convenient cop-out. We think that, since we "hired" our ministers to talk about religion, all we have to do is pay their salary and the job is done.

In a congregation near us where we sometimes worship, they have a bunch of tiny tots I affectionately call "the rug rats." They worship in that congregation because a few of the parents talked about their church at the local nursery school. They didn't grab other parents by the collar and say, "You gotta come to our church, see!" They were enthusiastic about their church so it came up naturally in their conversation.

One of my favourite parts of the worship service is coffee or tea afterwards. For me, the service isn't over until I follow the smell of coffee and sincerely ask a few people "How are you?" And some of them ask me the same question with the same sincerity. And I like coffee time because I get to exchange a bad joke with John and give Ray a bad time about his ties. It's the kind of exchange guys use as a way of saying, "I like you and I care about you."

Coffee time after church gives us an opportunity to practise what we preach. It's one of the times we learn how to ask genuinely caring questions. These caring questions open the door to the two-way sharing of faith.

There have been occasions when someone was welcomed during the worship service, but during the coffee time afterwards was left standing alone while everybody else is chatting with their friends. That shouldn't happen! As a layperson in my congregation, it is my job to make sure that new person feels welcome and valued.

The caring community

Most of us have had the experience of meeting someone and saying "Hi, Jason. How are things?" You see a moment of hesitation, a flicker of pain behind his eyes, before he says, "Oh fine, fine."

You know something is bothering Jason and you find it a bit embarrassing. So you tell yourself that Jason doesn't want to talk about whatever is troubling him. It's best to talk about the weather.

But isn't there something we could say or do that would at least let Jason know we'd be willing to share his pain if that's what he'd like?

There is.

Not long ago, I ran into a friend at the airport. I had heard about some really heavy problems in his life. So I gave him an extra long hug. "How about a cup of coffee?" I suggested. After a bit of small talk, he said, "You know, don't you? I could tell by the way you hugged me."

I don't usually know what to say to people when I realize they're hurting. It's taken me many years to free myself up enough to give hugs or to take someone's hand, rather than

always dishing out unwanted advice. Knowing how to say or do the appropriate thing comes naturally to some. Most of us have to consciously expose ourselves to situations where we can learn. I learned how to hug by being hugged when I was hurting.

Which is not to say we should go around hugging anybody who stands still for a moment. Indiscriminate hugging can be offensive. It can be interpreted as a sexual overture. It never hurts to ask if a hug would be welcome.

Learning how to show love

We learn what's helpful and appropriate in hugging, listening, hand-holding, and helping by being together and learning in small groups. These might be Bible study groups, social issue groups, marriage enrichment, or personal growth groups, Christian lifestyle groups, and many other kinds of gatherings.

In these groups, people share their own lives and listen to the stories others tell. They learn how to connect those stories with the foundational story, the story of a loving, creating God who acts in our lives. Some people expect God to speak to them through a lightning bolt, or a loudspeaker in the sky, or a particularly vivid dream. But God most often chooses to speak to us through the life or the voice or the caring of someone we know.

This more intimate gathering in small groups has helped thousands of us discover how to be more sensitive and open in the hundreds of interactions we have each day at work, at home, and at the shopping centre. It's in those conversations, that the Word of God is most effectively communicated.

That's evangelism. It's not the only kind, but it's certainly the most effective. Christians spread their faith around the world, not because they sent out professionals, but because

ordinary people like you and me lived and talked about their faith in the ordinary places where they worked and played.

Words and jargon

You are an evangelist when you help another person move closer to God. It may involve holding a hand or listening to a story. It may mean fighting the injustice that holds people down. It may include telling a simple story from our own life's journey.

It doesn't mean using all sorts of religious words or jargon. It doesn't need the high-sounding theological language of traditional liturgy or the equally structured "Jesus talk" of the fundamentalist. It needs the kind of talking Jesus did – simple, everyday, ordinary language, often without any religious words at all. Check the stories Jesus told in the Bible, especially in Matthew, Mark, and Luke, to see what I mean. His stories are simple, short, and beautiful.

God often communicates without the use of any language at all. I've experienced God's Spirit in the caring hand of someone who reached out and touched my life. That's why it is so desperately important that all of us really live out the concept of the caring community. When we express our love and caring for another person, we are (as we say to the children) "being God's helpers."

That's evangelism.

A minority group

I'm a member of the United Church because I believe that the people in my denomination hear the call of God clearly and respond with integrity (for the most part). That's not a put-down of anyone else. But if I felt it was happening more often or more faithfully in another community, I would join them.

Since I do have those feelings about the United Church, I

need to share them with others. But, in order to do that effectively, I've got to realize that I'm swimming upstream.

Christianity is no longer the standard by which society operates. I doubt if it ever really was. Active, involved Christians are now a minority group. And the United Church, even though it's the largest Protestant denomination in Canada, is no longer the "establishment" church. We are a splinter group on the edges of society. We have no built-in credibility.

But that's not all bad.

Digging out the answers

If being Christian no longer offers us status, or business connections, or social prestige, then we have some tough questions to ask. Why do I want to be part of this church anyway? There's no social or financial advantage. People will not think less of me if I don't belong. In fact, the reverse is probably true. So why do we have churches and why would I want to belong?

When you start working through those kinds of issues, you're starting to ask questions about what the church's mission really is. Is it to build a more beautiful building than the denomination down the street? Is it to pay off the mortgage? Is it to keep the kids off the street? Is it there to help me get away from the cares and worries of the world? To find comfort and friendship? To help me feel good? To bring me personal salvation? Life after death? Is it a base camp from which to take a run at the world's problems?

Is it all of the above? Or none? What is a church for, anyway?

Sometimes, congregations decide to take a serious look at those questions. They organize a series of study sessions, hold a weekend retreat, or bring in a facilitator to help them look at who they are and who they want to become. That can result in

something called a "mission statement," an expression of what a congregation is really about and who God is calling them to be. It's a good way to correct the drift that happens when you just go along without ever asking, "Where are we going? And why?"

It doesn't hurt to do this at the personal level as well. For me, the church provides a way of finding meaning in a life that often seems to offer very little of purpose and worth. In the church, I've gradually come to realize that God does love me, that I can see this love lived out in the life of Jesus Christ, and that the caring people of the church can give me a sense of belonging and strength.

Like most United Church people I came into the church looking for help. I came out of loneliness. I was finding my work as a radio open-line host meaningless. I was a newly married father, not really knowing how to cope with that either.

Having received help, and because I continue to find help, I want to return the favour. I want to help others.

Different approaches

Many congregations in the United Church become innovative and develop exciting programs and mission work that makes sense in their area. In hundreds of United Church congregations across Canada, people are involved in the Meals-on-Wheels program. They take a hot dinner to people, many of them senior citizens, who no longer cook for themselves.

Some work to support women's shelters or halfway houses for people who have been in jail. Some friends of ours retrieve polyester pants from the thrift shop. These pants can't be recycled, so they turn them into quilted blankets, which they give to halfway houses.

Hundreds of congregations offer nursery school facilities

and many include daycare. A few offer programs where young-sters who might otherwise be "latchkey kids" can go to the church at lunch time and before or after school.

Many people get involved in moral and social issues that most of our society has never adequately considered before: family violence, sexism, racism, homophobia, ecology, First Nations issues, militarism, third-world justice, AIDS, urban development, agricultural land use, and other questions that will determine the kind of life we'll have on this planet.

But the church is not just another advocacy group. We have a very special answer to the question, "Why should we be do-ing this?" Some very fine theologians have shown us that in some mysterious and holy way, the universe is God's body. When we defile this planet with our greed, we defile the body of God!

Reaching out

Christian perspectives get translated into action, and church groups (and Christians as individuals) often get out there to try to solve some of the problems.

Some big city congregations reach out to help people on skid row – the "hookers" the "druggies," the "winos." Jesus did the same kind of thing.

Some, like my home congregation, run a thrift shop where second-hand clothes are recycled. It's not only good ecology; it provides a place where all of us can find inexpensive clothing for ourselves and our kids. And, in the process, we raise money to help others in our town and overseas. Thrift shops regularly give money to a variety of causes, both in the church and out-side of it. A very nice fringe benefit is the sense of community among those who volunteer there.

As I write this, church people of many denominations are

deeply involved in helping Syrian refugees find a home here in Canada, and sending money to help disaster victims in various parts of the world.

Many people do their Christian worship and work outside of the church. For many years, the most respected politician in our city was a man who struggled hard with questions of ethics, morality, and justice in our area. His concerns came directly out of his Christian convictions, though he didn't say this when sitting around the city council table. And he was in church every Sunday because, as he said in the men's group one day, "it gives me a basis on which I can think clearly about what is right and what is wrong."

There's a tendency in some congregations to imply that the only way you can live your faith is to serve on a bunch of committees. That's a good way of doing it for some people. But it's not for me, nor for many others.

It's through my involvement with the church – through conversations, songs, prayers, sermons, hard work, and delightful play – that I sense where God is leading me.

The national church

Many churches work together through regional groupings and at the national level on a fantastic variety of mission programs.

But those programs struggle because there seems to be a strong trend to see the work of the church as local. "Our mission field is right outside our front door!" some leaders are saying.

That's a very narrow view. Yes, our mission field is right outside our door, but that door opens to the whole world where everything is interconnected. I can buy a new shirt for a few dollars because somebody in the third world gets paid only a few cents to make it.

As we focus our attention on local mission and as our giving moves more and more to the local congregation, the national or regional church is less and less able to take an active role in social change. That may be inevitable, but I deeply regret it.

At all levels, the United Church spends a great deal of money helping people in need. Some of the money goes to find out why that need exists so that root causes can be addressed.

The first part is easier and more popular than the second. Nobody can argue with helping a child in trouble. But when we start to ask questions like, "Why is that child in trouble?" we may get some answers that make us squirm.

We may find the child suffers from Fetal Alcohol Syndrome because of a drinking mother, or is desperately insecure because of a boozing, abusive father. Part of the problem may be liquor advertising. Is that child's father a failed athlete, who watches beer ads during a hockey game on TV, ads that imply he can be a real jock if he drinks enough beer? What happens to the child at the end of the game when daddy is tanked up and frustrated?

That's just one of the many issues the United Church continues to tackle, at local, regional, and national levels. If that falls by the wayside, it will be a huge loss.

We need to keep working on social justice issues even when we run into flack from business and government. When it might cut into somebody's profit, people often tell the United Church to back off. It seems that everyone is in favour of social justice and good ecology as long as somebody else picks up the tab. And as long as it doesn't affect my bottom line or my standard of living.

Deeper answers

The problems we face on the local scene tend to have their counterparts on the international scene.

When Bev and I were sent to the Philippines in the 1960s, we worked for the Filipino church. My job was to help develop a radio station that could tell people about new techniques of food production, family health care, and cottage crafts. It didn't take us long to realize the problem went far deeper than a lack of skills. The whole system of international trade was causing the basic problem.

For instance, one of the cottage industries we tried to help was wood carving, something Filipinos are famous for. But it seemed that no matter how hard they worked, or how well they did the job, the wood carvers always wound up with the same little bit of money in their pockets; just enough to stay barely alive.

When we came back to Canada from the Philippines, I saw one of those carvings in a department store selling for $35. That same carving sold in the markets of Manila for 5 pesos, about $1.25 Canadian, at that time. But the person who put about a week of hard work into the carving got one peso (25 cents). Everyone made a good profit in the system, except the one who did most of the work and who needed the money the most.

You don't have to spend much time studying the facts of international development before you come to a couple of very fundamental conclusions. One is that the gap between the rich and the poor is getting wider. Most of us here in Canada are getting richer. Most of them are getting poorer.

The second is that it really doesn't matter how much aid we send overseas, nothing is really going to change until we re-work a system that stacks the whole world's economic deck in

our favour. That means we've got to keep ourselves informed through careful and critical reading of the news media, and, if possible, through alternative media that are not as closely tied to the commercial system.

TV or not TV

Plenty of United Church people support mission and evangelism projects promoted by other agencies. They respond quickly to TV fund-raising spectaculars and slick promotional techniques, especially when someone shows the pleading eyes of a dying child. When the announcer assures us that all our money goes to the child – hardly any goes to administration – we're hooked.

Who paid for the advertisements? It costs mega bucks to produce such advertisements. Why didn't that money go to the child? And why is the child starving in the first place?

Church people think with their hearts. That's good. But we need to think with our heads, too, or we're an easy mark for any promoter with a good story.

The United Church is caught between a rock and a hard place. On the one hand, people who try to tell the story of the Church's outreach don't want to play on our emotions. On the other hand, few of us really respond to facts. We respond to people. We respond with our emotions, whether we admit that or not.

My personal view is that the United Church leans a bit more to facts and figures than it should, and that more "people stories" could be told. But that's a judgment call.

I do think that if more United Church people took the trouble to understand, they'd be willing to invest in the less glamorous but longer lasting attempts at solutions undertaken by our national church.

Biblical politics

It's hard to explain why church people get involved in things that sound more political or economic than religious. Shouldn't they stick with spiritual matters and leave politics and economics to people who know something about that?

Absolutely. Except that politics and economics are very spiritual matters. Read the Bible. It's full of politics. Jesus is constantly talking about money. "Where your treasure is, that's where your heart is," he says. Where you spend your money indicates what you think is most important. And whatever you think is most important is your religion.

If you want to find out what my religion really is, look at my Visa bill. There is a sense in which everything we do, and everything we don't do, is both political and religious.

The printed word

One way the story of the church's mission and evangelism effort is told is through *Mandate*, a magazine published at the national church offices in Toronto. It's good reading and probably the best way to keep in touch with what's happening in the church's outreach.

Mandate is available on subscription and it's sent to the clergy and other leaders in the congregation. It's a good magazine, but doesn't get into the hands of church members as much as it should.

The United Church Observer brings us news of what the church is doing and saying in its mission and evangelistic work. And each Sunday, in many churches, someone reads a "Minute for Mission" focusing on one of the church's local, national, or international outreach programs.

The Web

The United Church is doing some good things on the web. All the conferences and presbyteries are online, as is the national United Church. Those websites will provide you with all kinds of interesting links to the various parts of the church.

There are some who feel the future of the church may be electronic – that we'll eventually stop coming together in congregations and do all of that online. Similar predictions were made when radio first came along, and for television, too.

It didn't happen then, and I don't think it will happen with the Internet. In fact, "online church" may be an oxymoron – a self-contradicting term. To me, a church is a church only when "two or three are gathered" (to quote Jesus). The key word is "gathered," when we can look into each other's eyes and offer hands and hugs when needed.

New research is showing that the social and psychological benefits of religion happen when people come together to work, to pray, and to have fun. So-called "social media" may actually stifle community.

Which is not to say that some really interesting things won't happen online. They are worth checking out. Many, perhaps most, congregations have a website. Some are very actively reaching out through social media such as Facebook and Twitter.

The spiritual energy crisis

Still, too much of the story is left untold. At all levels of the church, evangelism is way down on the priority list, and that, I'm convinced, is one of the reasons we are a church in trouble.

We can't rely on the secular news media to tell our story. The media rely on hard news – news that almost by definition involves conflict. Somebody must say something that someone else disagrees with. And there must be a strong personality

who can be featured in a video clip or a sound bite or quoted in the paper, or tweeted.

Most church news is soft news. It doesn't make the secular news media or social media. But thousands of United Church people (and many others) are living courageous, faith-filled lives in the daily grind of suburban living.

Theirs are the stories we tell each other over coffee, and sometimes from the pulpit and in our church media. Those stories, of lives lived in faith, are our greatest natural resource and the answer to our spiritual energy crisis.

7

Reverend Sir or Madam

We have gifts that differ according to the grace given to us…
Romans 12:6

Tom was cutting up a bit as he handed out the bulletins on Sunday morning at our church.

"Programs! Programs!" he called in a twangy nasal singsong. "You can't tell who's the preacher without a program. Programs! Get yer programs!" And a few newcomers wondered if they had stumbled into a football game instead of a church service.

Actually, Tom was on to something. In the United Church, it can sometimes be hard to tell who is clergy and who isn't. It gets even harder when you try to tell an outsider the differences between an ordained minister, a diaconal minister, and a layperson. Not to mention designated lay ministers.

So hang on to your hats.

When is a minister a minister?

One of the things we need in this denomination is a lesson in down-to-earth language. We have problems with the words "minister" and "ministry."

The average person in the pew knows what the words mean, but our church leaders keep trying to tell us what they *ought* to mean. Any linguist knows that words mean what they mean to a group of people and the only thing you'll get trying to change that is heartburn.

Most of us would say that a "minister" is the person who does the preaching, the baptizing, the burying. The work this person does is "ministry." Simple.

But there are many lay people in the church who have been saying, "Hey! Most of what the ministers do is what we also do; caring about people; trying to bring a bit of justice and love into the world; spreading the good news. Clergy may do that professionally in the church, but many of us are doing it out there in hard-knock country. It's no easier."

Our church doesn't like putting people in order of rank. The "ministry" I have as a layperson is officially considered by the church to be just as important and significant as that of an ordained minister.

Officially. There are various things in the structure and rules of the church that show the United Church doesn't really believe this "official" word. Very few people, lay people or clergy, act as if it were true. But it's a nice thought.

Changes afoot

So I'm going to stick to the popular use of the word. When I say "minister," or "clergy," I mean the people who used to wear their collars backward. And I include in that category diaconal

ministers, designated lay ministers, and the assorted other categories of folk who work professionally in congregations. Or to use the jargon, people in "paid accountable ministry."

As I write this, the church is in the process of changing a whole bunch of things, including all these various categories of professional ministry. It's entirely possible, that by the time you read this, everything that follows will have changed.

For example, there's a proposal under consideration to put all those kinds of ministers into a blender and emulsify them into one category. It'll be interesting. If that has already happened, you can save yourself the trouble of reading the rest of this chapter.

Actually, no. There's lots here that will still apply.

The good, the bad, and the so-so

Here's what is in place as I write this.

The United Church doesn't like saying that clergy are better or holier than the rest of us. That's just as well, because they aren't. I probably know as many clergy (from many different denominations) as any layperson, to say nothing of being married to one. They come in as many varieties, sizes, degrees of goodness and badness, levels of intelligence, and styles of Christian commitment as do lay people.

Every minister knows this and many lay people know it, too. But there are some, often those who don't know "The Rev" very well, who expect clergy to hover six inches off the ground. They think clergy should be well above all the problems and temptations that plague those of us who are mere mortals.

I actually had one guy at a service club wonder out loud how it was that a female minister (in this instance, my wife, Bev) could get pregnant!

Few people are that naïve, but we often lay a pretty heavy trip on clergy. Those who try to live up to this "heavenly calling" either spend most of their life play-acting, or they suffer a severe breakdown.

Most clergy I know try to live decent, moral lives the same way other Christians do. They are bothered by the double standards of folk who think some behaviour is okay for them, but not for clergy. If some behaviour is "wrong," it's just as wrong for the person who visits the back pew once a year as it is for the minister.

Clergy don't necessarily "succeed" any better than the rest of us at personal morality, family happiness, successful financial management, and all the other things our society tells us are important. What most clergy *do* have is a strong faith. They have roots in the Christian community that help them deal with these problems more creatively. And they have a theological education that helps them see the ethical and social issues in our society.

Zero tolerance

No matter how you slice it, clergy have a strong influence and sometimes power in the congregation and in the community. They are looked up to, and trusted. Which is good, except that there have been a few church leaders (very few) who have abused that trust and have taken advantage of people.

Not too many years ago, we swept these situations under the rug. Now, we try to bring them out in the open and deal with them.

The United Church has zero tolerance around sexual abuse by church leaders, whether these be clergy or lay. We're encouraged to blow the whistle, quickly and hard.

If you have such a concern and don't know where else to go

with it, phone the personnel minister of your conference. (See the Appendix for a list of conference offices and contact information.) You can also find this information on the United Church website: www.united-church.ca.

Ordination and commissioning

What sets clergy apart in the life of the church is their training for a particular kind of work. No, that's not really the heart of it, because a layperson could have the same training. Some lay people do.

What sets clergy apart is ordination – and commissioning – the "laying on of hands" by a conference of the United Church, and dedicating the person to a vocation in the ministry. Then there are designated lay ministers, who often do the same kind of work as those who are ordained or commissioned.

Lay ministers

In an earlier edition of this book, I predicted that more and more lay people would become involved in ministry. That has happened, and I think that the number of lay people involved in ministry will continue to increase.

We may become more and more like the early church, when there was very little organized structure and people met in homes to eat together, to pray, and to share their joys and struggles. These groups had leaders, but they were not paid by anyone. They simply did this because they felt called into this kind of ministry.

In the United Church, lay people can lead in worship and preach. They can even conduct funerals. Whether they have the skills to do these things is, of course, another question.

I'm a layperson. I often lead worship and preach when clergy in our area are sick or away. But I don't have most of the skills

and training to do the kind of pastoral and leadership work a congregation needs. I'm not qualified for the kind of work ministers do.

Many congregations employ lay people to do Christian education and other kinds of work. They may be full-time and salaried. Many of our overseas missionaries are lay people. A high proportion of the staff in various church offices are lay people. In addition, there are lay people like myself who are not employed by the church, but who are in full-time Christian work.

To confuse the issue a bit more, there are clergy who don't work in congregations. They work in hospitals, prisons, as part of university chaplaincies, or they teach at theological schools. Some do administrative work in national church and conference offices.

So what's the difference? When it's possible for two people to be in identical jobs but one is a "Rev" and the other isn't, it gets so you really can't tell the preachers without a program.

As far as I can tell, the basic difference is that clergy, ordained and commissioned, are "in orders." It's not so much about who takes orders from whom. Those in "ordered" ministry are "set aside" and "designated" for ministry. They make promises – a commitment – to act as leaders in the church. They are accountable in a way that lay people are not. In the United Church, they are subject to the direction of their presbytery, which is a gathering of all the churches in a particular area.

The staff team

There's an important church vocation that's often overlooked – the secretary, or in some cases, the church administrator. A good secretary can be as important to the functioning of the church as the minister. The secretary often is the one person who knows

who's who, what's what, where's which, and why things are done the way they are. Or aren't.

The minister, by the way, is not supposed to double as the church secretary. The congregation is required to provide "adequate secretarial assistance." Some congregations (especially the larger ones) have an administrator on staff – someone who looks after all the nuts and bolts of running a congregation.

Caretakers are also important members of the staff team. Whether paid staff or volunteer, caretakers make a very substantial contribution to the atmosphere of a church, and that is important. They not only need to know how to keep the church clean, but they need people skills. They relate to the many volunteers and folks from outside organizations who use the facilities.

Some large congregations have full-time musicians who conduct the choir and provide all the music. But this is rare. In most congregations it's a volunteer position, though some get a small honorarium.

The organist/pianist or music director (this could be one or two people) is a key person in the planning of the Sunday morning service. If the music leader and the minister are going off in different directions, the service becomes a hodgepodge and the music becomes a performance, rather than a contribution to worship.

A day in the life of the "Rev"

Many of us lay people have very little idea what goes into a minister's week. We go to church on Sunday morning and often assume that getting the worship service ready and preaching is all the minister really does.

Certainly, preparing the service takes hard and creative work. Even though I've had a ringside seat (being married to a minis-

ter), I didn't realize how hard it was until I acted as a stand-in when my own congregation was between ministers.

It was great for the first couple of weeks. But it wasn't long before I heard the sound of my own fingernails scraping the bottom of the idea barrel. And all I had to do was the preaching. I did none of the pastoral or administrative work that clergy usually do.

Let me tell you, preparing that service week after week, especially the sermon, is hard, hard work!

Ministerial duties

As a professional writer, my opinion is that a good sermon takes at least three full days to write. That's what it takes me. But I've never yet met a minister who could set aside that kind of time.

"So, except for yakking for an hour on Sunday, ministers don't do much. What a cushy job!" I heard that comment a few years ago, and came close to being charged with assault.

Many clergy work hard at administration – keeping the organization functioning. They become the chief executive officer of the congregation, particularly if it's a large one. That may involve endless meetings. I've sometimes wondered why more congregations don't hire an administrator and leave clergy to do the work they're trained for.

Many clergy also lead study groups. They can't just come into those groups cold. Preparation usually takes longer than the meeting time.

Pastoral work usually takes up a large slice of the minister's time. That includes visiting people in hospitals, calling on people who can't get out, visiting new families, getting in touch with families who are having trouble, planning funerals and weddings, and...you get the picture.

Often, it means people coming to the minister's office look-

ing for help with a personal problem. Most of us have no idea how often the phone rings in the minister's office or at their home. People dream up some trivial reason for phoning and wind up unburdening themselves about a problem. It's been said that the telephone is the Protestant confessional.

"What took you so long?" I demanded of Bev several years ago when she was still in active ministry. She'd gone to get the mail. That should take 15 minutes. Then I noticed that she looked rather pale and shaken. She had spent the time with a man who had, quite literally, wiped the remains of his best friend off the floor after a shotgun suicide.

A kind, informed friend

I have a strong impression more and more people are going to clergy for help. It may be part of a general recognition that the problems we encounter in life are physical, psychological, so-cial, *and* spiritual, all woven together. Or it may just be that the price is right – usually nothing at all.

But clergy don't have the time, and often lack the training, to do in-depth counselling. Wise clergy quickly refer people to medical or counselling pros. People who think they can get through life on their own strength and intelligence are usually kidding themselves.

I've found clergy were most helpful to me in my problems when they acted as a kind, well-informed friend who could point me to the place where I could get the specific help I needed. In other words, when they acted as a referral service.

Another big item in the clergy time budget relates to the many group activities within the congregation, including per-haps the Sunday school, midweek youth and/or adult groups, and even some groups only marginally connected with the church.

Many ministers find themselves spending great amounts of time finding leaders, getting groups fixed up with the right kinds of material, encouraging leaders when they feel discouraged, and, hardest of all, figuring out how to ease an inept volunteer out of a position without hurting their feelings.

Because the church operates mostly on volunteers, few ministers can demand anything. They have to rely on tact, diplomacy, people's good will, and the grace of God. Especially the grace of God.

Multi-meetings

Doing all that involves meetings. Because most church people have daytime jobs, the meetings are in the evening. So clergy often wind up spending their days at the office and their nights at meetings. It can be a killer.

On top of that are funerals, which seem to come in bunches and at the most inconvenient times. Clergy usually take their pastoral work seriously, which may mean several visits to the grieving family, plus the funeral service itself. And they often do follow-up visits with those who are grieving. What most of us forget is that often, when the person who dies is a member of the congregation, the minister is also one of the mourners.

And then there are weddings. Not nearly as many as there used to be. They involve at least one interview with the couple and probably several more pre-marital counselling sessions and a wedding rehearsal.

And baptismal interviews, to make sure the parent(s) of the baby know what is involved. And…

Back in the "good old days," ministers thought nothing of working a 60- or 70-hour week. They sacrificed their family and their health for the church. Most clergy don't want to do that anymore. They want a life the same way you and I do. Their

spouses and children and friends want some time with them, too. The stress all this brings on can easily result in burnout.

"Our former minister used to mow the lawn in summer and shovel snow in winter!" someone complained to the new minister.

"I know," said the new minister. "I talked to your former minister on the phone. He doesn't want to do it anymore."

Community ministry

Many clergy feel that to have an effective ministry they should be involved in community work. So they become chaplain for the Legion, or run for the town council or school board, or they become active in the local mental health association. The local community is also a good place to meet new people, do some grassroots evangelism, and build community partnerships. Some congregations, especially in smaller centres, encourage their clergy to be leaders in the community.

A number of years ago, I met a minister who was sent to a town where the church had died but hadn't been buried. "I join everything in sight and talk to everybody I meet. Maybe that way I'll make enough contacts so that we can breathe a bit of life back into the church." He called it "mouth-to-ear resuscitation" for a dying church.

United Church clergy often take the lead in ecumenical relationships – working with other denominations in the community in social justice ministries, hospital chaplaincy, and just plain neighbourliness.

It can be very easy to overdo that kind of community involvement. And when you come right down to it, it's not the minister who represents the church in the community. It's you and me. The clergy can help us learn how to do that. But it's really our job.

Occupational hazards

Some people expect the minister to know everybody and everything about anything that's going on in the church. That can be true in a very tiny congregation, but not when there's more than a handful of members. Clergy who try to live up to that kind of expectation tend to get a bit squirrely. Besides, that's not their job.

It's the people of the congregation who are responsible for the life and work of the church. The minister is their resource person. It's not the other way around.

The minister ought to know, generally, what's going on. At least about the main activities. But it's a healthy thing for clergy to be quite clueless about who is locking up after the meeting or whether the phone bill got paid last month.

Clergy should work hard at *not* knowing how to fix anything around the church. They should never know where anybody put anything. And they should make it a point of not knowing when and where all the meetings and events are taking place. They don't need to sing in the choir (unless they really want to) or bake the best apple pies. A clergy friend grins when she tells me she practises "selective incompetence. I don't even know where the furnace room is!"

I know what it's like trying to have a family dinner when the phone keeps ringing with folks calling to find out the when and where of events and meetings – information which was all there in the previous Sunday's bulletin.

Wise clergy are very selective about what they admit to knowing, but they do not enjoy being clueless about things like who is in the hospital, or sick at home, or where trouble is brewing in the church.

"Why didn't you come and see me when I was in the hospital?" people will sometimes ask their minister.

"I didn't know you were in the hospital. Nobody told me."

"Well, I thought you'd just know," they tell the minister. I can tell you for sure that clergy are totally incompetent when it comes to reading crystal balls. Nor are they much good at reading people's minds. Anyway, in many cases, hospital visiting is done by dedicated lay people.

The reality is that many hospitals no longer list a person's religious affiliation on their admission forms. Even when they do, people leave that space blank. And more and more, hospitals are zipping people in and out so there's no time for a visit.

When I went in for a hernia repair, the only reason I got a visit from my minister is because she was my wife and had to come and take me home.

The care and feeding of clergy

Burnout and rust-out are two occupational hazards for clergy. The people of the congregation have some responsibility to help clergy avoid these problems.

Clergy are often their own worst enemies when it comes to burnout. They have a high sense of vocation. Some are just plain workaholics who think an 80-hour week is normal. Some have job descriptions that not even a certified saint would be able to manage.

Ministry and Personnel Committees in the congregation should be able to help the minister learn to say "No." Sometimes they can take the message to the congregation that they didn't hire Superman or Wonder Woman. Occasionally, the committee may need to come down hard on clergy who have the kind of commitment that can hide a self-destructive instinct.

Rust-out is a more serious problem. It's also more subtle. It's what happens to clergy (and to you and me), when they don't pay attention to their own spiritual lives. In the same way

that we all become physically run down if we don't pay attention to our diet and exercise, we become spiritually run down if we don't do those things that build spiritual muscles.

Clergy, of course, are specially trained in spiritual development. That's their vocation, and they often do a good job of counselling us lay people in this necessary art. But they often don't practise what they preach.

Ministry is one of the toughest jobs going. Just dealing with the personalities in any congregation is a full-time job. Every congregation has these people – from opinionated old-timers to enthusiastic newcomers, from archconservatives to archliberals, from the very elderly to the very young, from single parents to extended families. People in a huge spectrum of social and psychological situations. Each of them wants the minister to meet their specific needs.

Clergy need to use their built-in safety valves and we, as members of the congregation, need to make sure they do. A United Church minister is expected to take a month of paid holiday and three weeks study leave each year. That's not up to the congregation to decide. That's in the rules. The Ministry and Personnel Committee should insist that both be used for their intended purpose. Also, clergy, like many other professionals, have access to a sabbatical leave after five years. They need to take it.

Do your minister a favour. Ask, "What are you doing on your study leave this year? Are you due for a sabbatical?" If you get consistent waffling or some mumble about there not being time, take it up with your Ministry and Personnel Committee. It's their job to insist that holidays, study leave, and sabbaticals are used fully. And the congregation should put at least some of the cost of that study leave in the annual budget.

It's essential!

Vacations help prevent burnout. Study leaves and sabbaticals help prevent rust-out.

Coming and going

In the United Church, the minister is not "the boss" of a congregation. But neither is a congregation "the boss" of the minister, even though they pay the salary. The two are supposed to work together.

But, if push comes to shove, it's important to know that the minister is placed in the congregation by the presbytery. And a congregation can't dismiss a minister without the involvement of the presbytery to which it belongs.

There are special words for hiring and firing in the United Church. A minister is "called," or "appointed." That's the "hiring" part. And, when the minister leaves, for whatever reason, the presbytery "declares a vacancy."

Actually, the word "called" is used for a very good reason. When a minister comes to serve a congregation, there is far more involved than simply making sure the qualifications match the salary and benefits. God is part of the process. The "call" comes not just from the congregation. It comes from God.

That call, by the way, is no excuse for expecting the minister to work for peanuts. The clergy are also professional people and should be paid as such. And they have the same physical needs as every other mortal.

When a congregation needs a minister, it's not a matter of putting a "help-wanted" ad in a magazine or on the web, although a congregation may well do that. The presbytery is involved from day one and helps the congregation through what can seem like a long and complicated process.

All shapes and sizes

The United Church probably has more varieties of clergy than any other Canadian denomination. That's great! The problem is that many congregations, when considering a new minister, go for the "standard brand" and don't realize that a different style of clergy can be a breath of fresh air.

I think it's delightful and interesting that we have so many clergy varieties: women and men of various ethnic backgrounds, sexual orientations, gender identities, ages, physical challenges, assets, and interests.

A congregation that calls a minister who is not the ordinary garden variety clergy is often rewarded with new insights and creativity.

Stereotypes

Fortunately, in the United Church, we've eliminated many of our stereotypes. Few of us have an image of the minister as the befuddled old parson drinking tea with old ladies, even though the TV sitcoms love to perpetuate that idea. There are still a few who assume the minister is an authority on everything. That comes from the days when the clergy were among the few educated people in town.

The worst clergy stereotype, one that lives more outside the church than in it, is of the totally out-of-it parson. This minister has never heard a four-letter word, is offended at the mere mention of booze, thinks sex is a number that comes after five, and is some kind of saint who never has to deal with the pressures and temptations the rest of us face.

The clergy I know are down-to-earth worldly people. They are as aware of what happens on the seamy side of life as social workers or bartenders. Often, the work they do has them dealing with situations that would curl your hair.

A fire in the belly

If you are thinking of entering the ordered ministry, explore it carefully. It's not an easy life. Go for it if you've got a "fire in your belly" and you don't want to do anything else. Talk to your minister first, and then if you feel "called," your minister will arrange a meeting with the governing body of your home congregation.

If you haven't been involved in a congregation, the first thing you need to do is become active for at least a couple of years. Then think about turning pro.

If you and your church board feel God is calling you into professional ministry, then they will help you find a "discernment committee," a group of people who will meet with you a number of times over the course of year or so, to help you ask the right kinds of questions and help you think and pray your way to a sense of certainty about your call. That long, involved process doesn't always sit well with people who have a strong sense of call to the ministry. They sometimes feel their sense of being called by God is the only thing that's important and they should be ordained immediately. The United Church says yes, this personal sense of call is of vital importance. It must be there. If it's genuine, it'll still be there through all the screening and training.

The United Church has a pretty good batting average at selecting clergy. It's not perfect. People often take great delight in telling you the story they heard about the minister who ran off with the organist. More often, they tell you about a minister who was a bit silly or insensitive in a particular situation.

But most of the stories you hear about clergy tell how they cared for, inspired, advised, and helped – how they provided a special kind of caring leadership through the "slings and arrows of outrageous fortune," to quote Shakespeare.

They also tend to have a great sense of humour.

LGBTQ clergy

In the 1980s, the United Church went through a long and painful struggle over whether homosexual persons could be ministers in the church. There's still some pain and misunderstanding. Older people like me have had to move a very long way in our understanding, and it's not been easy. For some, this has been very painful. But the issue is clear and settled. Homosexual persons who are in a loving relationship with another person, or single, just like heterosexual persons, can be ministers in our church.

From day one, back in 1925, the United Church has said that anyone who considers themselves a Christian can be a member of the United Church and all United Church people are eligible to be considered for the ordained or commissioned ministry. With that as a basic understanding, it was reasonable to conclude that if the various parts of the church all feel the person is theologically, socially, academically, psychologically, and morally fit to be a minister, then it's a go. Their sexual orientation or gender identity should not be an issue.

Some conservative denominations have torn a pretty wide strip off the United Church for its attitude toward homosexual, transgendered, and bisexual persons. Those denominations are hiding their heads in the sand. Every denomination in Canada has practising homosexual clergy. They stay well locked in their closets because coming out probably means they'd be kicked out of their church. Some of them have found spiritual refuge in the United Church. My own congregation has been deeply enriched by people from the LGBTQ community. They make a talented and enthusiastic contribution.

I am proud that my church had the courage to face the question head-on and to take the flak. We still have a long way to

go, and the walk is often painful. We've decided that nobody would be excluded from anything because of the way God made them.

I think we chose the right path!

A great bunch of people

Altogether, I think the United Church has perhaps the best, most flexible, relevant, and committed ministry of any denomination. Of course, I'm prejudiced. But if you get to know them, I'm sure you'll also find that they are a great bunch of women and men. And fun, too!

United Church clergy follow the grand traditions of the Bible, where God called some of the darnedest people to be prophets, leaders, and witnesses. None of them would survive if God's grace didn't help them over some of the rough spots and pickles they get themselves into. Of course, that's true of us lay people, too.

Most clergy find ministry in the local congregation an exciting and challenging vocation. Working with people who are involved because they want to be; learning to live in a community that needs their guidance and help and that offers them love in return; doing something their deepest convictions tell them is the most significant job in the world; that has got to be one of the world's finest vocations.

According to a *Time Magazine* special 2016 edition on *The Science of Happiness,* among all the various occupations, clergy are the most happy in their jobs. Poor gas station attendants are at the very bottom, and journalists, like me, just barely above the middle.

I don't know how you go about measuring a thing like "happiness," and I have met clergy who were very unhappy in their

chosen vocation. But of the many clergy I have known well, most of them were genuinely happy with their work and had a strong sense of being called by God.

The salary may not be great (though it's getting better), but the fringe benefits are fantastic.

8

How We Decide

The gifts Christ gave were that some would be apostles, some prophets, some evangelists, some pastors and teachers.
Ephesians 4:11 (NRSV, adapted)

I worked for the United Church for a while. Part of my job was "media relations." That meant I had to take reporters around to help them get their stories. Often it involved explaining the United Church to them.

One reporter was quite visibly shaken when I introduced her to the moderator (the highest elected position in the church), who was in the lunch lineup just ahead of us at a conference.

"Your moderator is in the lineup getting his own food like everybody else?" She found that very upsetting.

Often reporters would ask, "Who's in charge here? Who makes the decisions?"

"Well, we don't have any one person in charge," I'd say. "We work through a series of committees so that all those in-

volved can have their say in what we do." Reporters, it seemed, were not much impressed with that idea.

Nowadays, I often try to explain to my writer friends that the United Church is a "democratic and collegial organization." That's when I see their eyes rolling up into their heads. "Anyway," I say, "it's designed to deal with complicated moral and theological questions, questions about what is right and wrong and what God is saying to the church."

"Does it work?"

"No. Well, sometimes. But nobody's figured out a better way. It's a lot like a democratic government, which doesn't always work that well either and we'd scrap it, if there was a better alternative."

Of course, our kind of collegial church government carries a price tag. When you have a variety of people with strong convictions, all of them convinced they are being faithful to the call of God, you have a recipe for conflict.

Tough work ahead

The United Church has had more than its share of struggle in the last three decades. And, as I write this, it seems headed for some hard slogging, working out a radical reorganization to the whole national United Church structure.

The plain fact is that the kind of structure the church now has is way too expensive and we can't afford all the people it takes to do all the jobs. We simply can't operate that way anymore. We've got to simplify.

But I have no idea how long that'll take or how it'll come out in the wash. My crystal ball has gone off-line.

Keep your eye on *The United Church Observer*, the church's national magazine. Also check on the national church website: www.united-church.ca.

Don't rely too much on what you read or hear in the media. They tend to latch on to whatever element seems most controversial and they mostly interview people who have extreme reactions.

In fact, it's always good to be a bit skeptical about religious news in the secular news media.

So I'm going to say very little about how the United Church functions beyond the local congregation. But here's a very quick, and therefore oversimplified overview.

Presbytery

When the Methodist, Presbyterian (well, most of them), Congregational, and Union churches got together in 1925, they developed a form of church government they hoped would incorporate the best of their various different styles.

They decided that the presbytery would be one of the key units in United Church organization. It would do some of the things bishops do in other denominations, but it wouldn't be just one person. Presbytery would be a group of elected representatives, both clergy and lay, who would represent the various congregations in a geographical region.

Conference and General Council

Just as a congregation is part of a presbytery, the presbyteries are part of a larger geographically-defined conference, with one current exception – the All Native Circle Conference, which is open to aboriginal congregations and presbyteries across the country, though not all Indigenous congregations have chosen to be part of that conference. There are from two to 14 presbyteries in each of the 13 conferences.

Every three years, delegates from all across Canada get together for an event called the General Council. The delegates

are elected by conferences and are called "commissioners." It's at General Council meetings that national policies are hammered out, and the church as a whole declares itself.

The moderator

A new moderator is elected at each meeting of the General Council, which is usually every three years. The moderator is not like the pope or prime minister. Perhaps a little like the Governor General or the speaker in the House of Commons, though that's not quite accurate because moderators *do* take part in the church's decision making.

Any member of the United Church can hold any elected position. Lay and clergy, women and men, young and old, those in the LGBTQ community and people of different races have held them all, including the position of moderator.

Simplicity

So let's get down to talking about the local church.

There are some very small congregations where folks stand around after church on Sundays and decide whatever needs deciding. No committees. Everybody knows everything that's going on.

This works really well unless there's a strong personality or two that somehow manages to run everything. Then the whole thing becomes unworkable and sometimes very destructive.

The board

Medium-sized churches usually develop something that's half way between what follows and the tiny church I just mentioned. And they do it in a variety of creative ways. Most of them are variations on what follows.

All congregations in the United Church have a governing

body, sometimes called a unified or "official board," sometimes called a "council." It's elected by the congregation at an annual meeting. The council may also include members from various groups, such as the United Church Women, the men's group, the Christian education committee, the board of trustees, the finance committee, building committee, the youth organization, and others.

Most boards or councils meet once a month. Every committee of the congregation reports to it.

Some congregations have a more traditional form of organization based on two different groups: the "session" made up of "elders," and the "committee of stewards." The session looks after spiritual matters like baptisms, preaching, worship, Christian education, etc., and the stewards deal with money, the building, that sort of thing.

The minister, who is a member of presbytery and, therefore, not technically a member of the congregation, can be chair of the board or session. But most congregations feel it's wiser to have one of the church members serve as chair so the minister can participate more easily in decision making.

The minister, by the way, is an *ex officio* member of every committee. That means the minister has the right to attend any meeting of any committee in the church (except the Ministry and Personnel Committee), with or without an invitation. Most clergy are far too busy to even think about doing that.

Committees

There's quite a variety of ways in which boards organize themselves. Larger churches usually have five basic committees, though there are many variations on this theme.

The finance committee or the committee of stewards raises money for the church, presents a budget to the congregation

for approval, and supervises spending and general office administration. Some congregations put all or part of this responsibility onto the property committee.

The ministry and personnel committee (often referred to as M&P) deals with the many matters that come up in connection with having professional people on staff – clergy, secretaries, music leaders, caretakers, and others. The minister and other staff don't normally attend these meetings unless invited to discuss some particular matter.

The Sunday school committee is now usually called the Christian education committee (CE committee) or the Christian development committee, or the faith formation committee. Those name changes are significant. They represent a broader attitude to what education means in the congregation.

We're beginning to realize that education is a cradle-to-the-grave kind of thing. It's important to have a strong church school for kids. It's also important to have programs for the Christian development of teenagers and adults of every age, including those of us in the geezer category.

Since *The Whole People of God* and *Seasons of the Spirit* curricula came along, more and more churches are seeing education as something the whole congregation does together.

The fifth group is the worship and sacraments or spiritual life committee. Others simply call it the worship committee.

Related to it, and sometimes part of the same committee, is a concern for congregational life. By that we mean things like small group activities, social events, and things that build the sense of community. Such a group may organize hospital visits and visits to people in their homes. Sometimes there's an evangelism and communications committee somewhere in this mix. These groups have responsibility for the spiritual life of the congregation, how the Word of God is proclaimed and how it is

lived. This includes taking responsibility for the pastoral care of people.

The worship committee also decides on the style and content of the regular worship service. They, or the board as a whole, decide who will be baptized and married and they make many other decisions that are important to the life of the congregation. Unfortunately, far too many boards simply leave all these decisions up to the minister and go on to things that are less complicated.

And the board of trustees. Trustees have a kind of legal function which I only vaguely understand, but you can get all the info if you go to The United Church of Canada website: www.united-church.ca.

Spiritual and other stuff

It's these "spiritual" matters that the church considers most important. To be on the worship committee, you should, technically at least, be a full member of the church. In fact, you're not supposed to vote on spiritual matters in any meeting, not even a congregational meeting, unless you're a full member.

Adherents, those who may actively support the church but who haven't actually joined, may vote only on "temporal" matters like money and buildings. This is one of those rules that's ignored or stretched in many congregations, maybe even most of them. And there's some talk that it may be changed.

Communication

Evangelism and communications committees often have the job of doing things like newsletters, encouraging people to subscribe to *The United Church Observer,* and arranging for audiovisual equipment and supplies. In some places, this is called the congregational life committee.

They might also be responsible for analyzing what happens on a Sunday morning; whether people are made to feel welcome, whether the sound system works, and whether the building looks nice.

Most importantly, they establish and maintain contact with newcomers. They try to make them feel welcome and to get them involved in church life. When these matters are dealt with creatively, the church is strengthened and it's able to do God's work more efficiently.

The gospel calls us, not only to the fellowship of the church, but to reach out in love to others in the community and around the world. To do that, many congregations have two more committees. These committees have a variety of names in different congregations, but the responsibilities shouldn't be neglected. They are church in society, and world outreach.

These two committees are sometimes combined into one group because it's no longer possible to sort out which are international problems and which are strictly Canadian. The concerns are similar – justice, peace and the integrity of creation. It's the job of this committee, as it's the job of the whole church, to study and do something about the issues I will mention in Chapter 11.

Of course, some congregations have far more committees than the ones I've named. And some have far fewer. Many congregations simply don't have enough people for all those committees, so all of the church's business is handled by the whole board.

I don't know if it will become a trend or not, but some congregations have moved to what they call "passion groups." If someone has a passionate interest in something, that person is invited to gather others with similar feelings, and that becomes the "committee." And when the passion or the need is

no longer there, the passion group dissolves. Yes, of course the passion group folk check with the board before doing anything that would affect others in the congregation. Or at least they should.

Who's in charge here?

Every church and every religious group has some kind of organization and it's easy to spend time arguing which is best. To a large extent, the organization reflects the kind of people a church attracts.

Organizations that have authority spread up and down throughout the system tend to attract people who like to have a hand in running things. The United Church seems, for the most part, to be that kind of organization, though you can still find congregations where the leadership is very much from the top down.

The official position is that the Bible is the "primary source and ultimate standard of Christian faith and life" and that Jesus Christ is the "chief cornerstone." That's where the authority lies. It means that no one person in the church can ever claim to have the last word, which makes it much harder to get anything decided.

The collegial process

In the United Church, we believe that the Holy Spirit communicates both with individuals and with the whole community of God's people that is the gathered church. When we get together to make decisions, God is part of that process. What an individual believes must always be tested against what the whole church believes.

I don't know of any better way the church can be faithful. It is important that we do what we believe is right, not simply

what is popular. Government by opinion poll is not an option for a church that wants to be guided by the Holy Spirit.

My church home

I am intensely proud to be a member of The United Church of Canada. I am proud because of the quality of the people I find in it. I am proud to be part of a community that has the courage to act on principle; to do what they feel is right, even at great personal and organizational cost.

I am proud to be part of a community that includes people who don't stomp off in a snit when the church decides something with which they deeply and fundamentally disagree. It takes courage and commitment to stay in the family.

I am proud to be part of a church community that grows and changes and listens and struggles – that refuses to get caught in the stagnant waters of yesterday's issues and has the courage to swim upstream.

The United Church has a heritage of diversity, of openness, of refusing to be dogmatic. We have been an inclusive church, which means, among other things, that we include the people in our own church family with whom we radically disagree.

We use the word "inclusiveness" quite often. We really knew it was more than just a word when the United Church of Canada said that persons in the entire LGBTQ community must be fully welcome in the church to the point of being considered for ordered ministry.

Now, it must become more than just a word as we find ways of actively including and valuing people and congregations who feel they are trampled on and marginalized by our "inclusive" process.

If we fail – if either the far left or the far right or anyone else for that matter feels left out – we have contradicted our own

theology of inclusiveness. We will have denied the vision that created The United Church of Canada.

The struggle

We're not a perfect church. The democratic form of governance in the United Church works because most of the people all the way up and down the ladder are trying to live the gospel as they know it. It takes a lot of good will and openness to make it work.

Yes, some are clods and some are freeloaders. Some are sound asleep and there are a few rotten apples. There may even be a few who seem to be downright evil.

But most United Church people, lay and clergy, women and men, are committed to living and working out their faith as part of the whole church of Jesus Christ.

For that, I thank God!

9
Money

How does God's love abide in anyone who has the world's goods
and sees a brother or sister in need and yet refuses to help?
1 John 3:17

Money is considered a bad word by some people. At least, it's not a word we say out loud in church. Instead, we use words like "stewardship."

The definition of stewardship, in the church sense, is "what we do with what we've got." So stewardship certainly means more than money. It involves the way we use our time, our talents, our energy, our skills, the earth, and anything else we have. Including our physical bodies.

Still, our most important symbol of "what we've got" is money. So money is what I'm talking about in this chapter.

A down-to-earth faith

You can find lots of people who say the church should concentrate on spiritual things. I agree totally. And since the Bible talks a lot about money, money is one of those spiritual things we must talk about. There's a profound connection between our spiritual lives and our financial lives.

Jesus had plenty to say about money. So did other biblical writers. Check Deuteronomy 8:10–18, Matthew 19:16–29 and 1 Timothy 6:4–11, to name just a few.

Christianity is a very materialistic religion. "Worldly" things like sex, money, and politics are the very things it deals with. Some other major religions try to get you away from all that. "Salvation" becomes so "spiritual" that nasty things like money and sex and power simply don't affect you anymore.

But Christianity doesn't take you away from anything. Christianity plunks you right into the middle of life as you are living it, and helps you use what you have creatively. Our money and our sexuality are gifts of God.

As Christians, we do our best to live as Jesus lived, and Jesus got lots of bad press because he insisted on being involved with "earthly" things. Not that he was particularly concerned with people's wealth (unless it came at somebody else's expense). But he was very concerned about what people did with their wealth and power, with their time and talents, and with their bodies.

Most of all, he was concerned about their attitudes. "Where your treasure is," said Jesus, "there your heart will be also." In other words, when you take out your cheque book or your credit card, you are expressing your faith. Or lack of it.

It's important to talk about money. Otherwise, what we do with our dollars might contradict what we claim to believe. We've got to "put our money where our mouth is," as we used to say playing poker. "Put up or shut up!"

Both of those expressions should be applied to people in the church.

Ten percent off the top

In the Hebrew scriptures, the rule is that you give the first ten percent of everything to God. Off the top. Before deductions.

That's the way they did it in Bible times. At harvest time, if you had a hundred bushels of grain, the first thing you did was take ten bushels to the temple. It's called a "tithe."

That ten percent off-the-top figure was used at a time when most people thought they were doing well if they weren't starving.

In many of our Third World sister churches, where the standard of living is far lower than ours, people still take the Bible seriously. They give ten percent. They tithe.

Many of us in the United Church set aside our tithe (and yes, I'm talking about ten percent of everything that comes in) just as soon as the paycheque comes in. We may not give it all to the church, but we do give it away. We find that habit satisfying and liberating. Somehow, the rest of the budget problems seem to come into a better perspective when we tithe.

Unfortunately, we're a minority. I'm proud of the United Church in many ways, but I'm not a bit proud of the way most of us respond with our money. In Canada, people in our denomination are among the worst in terms of giving to the work of the church. We seem to be in a competition with the Anglicans to see who has the lowest per-capita giving.

On the other hand, a friend, a United Church member who does income tax returns for others, tells me that the folks who give significant amounts to the church also give far more to other causes. This is not true just in the United Church. All religiously active people tend to give more to non-religious organizations than those who are not active or who are less active.

The church is still suffering from the "buck-a-week" syn-

drome. I know people who have been coming to church for years and put a loonie on the plate every Sunday. Their salaries have been going up. All their other expenses have been going up. Their standard of living has been going up.

But the church keeps getting a buck a week.

Somebody wondered out loud what would happen if everybody in our congregation went on social assistance. Welfare. Then, if one person, just one person in each family would tithe, what would happen? In fact, the amount of money given to the church would actually increase.

I personally know United Church people on social assistance who tithe! I also know United Church people who live in homes worth several million, and who put in five dollars a week.

Sorry. That sounds like a bit of a rant. But it's true.

Pledging

Most congregations in the United Church encourage people to make a pledge at the beginning of the year. This involves looking at what we have and how we are doing, and then deciding how much we plan to give.

Having this information helps the congregation set its annual budget and it's the only sensible way a congregation can operate. Congregations must pay regular expenses such as salaries, building repairs, mortgages, and many other things. The board members who draw up the budget need to have a reasonable idea of what kind of income to expect.

It's not that much to ask. We make all sorts of financial commitments. We sign on the dotted line for car payments and mortgages and phones. And those are legally binding.

A church pledge isn't binding. It's a statement of intention. Nobody can predict the future, but we can all take a guess at what it's likely to be. That guess should be the basis of our

pledge. If we lose a job or wind up in the hospital or our spouse skips out, nobody would expect us to stick with it.

Making a pledge is simply one way we cooperate with the people we elect to manage our congregation. They're trying to do that in a sensible and fiscally sound manner. We wouldn't want them to do any less. So they need our cooperation.

Those people who say, "I'll give what I can," usually mean they'll give what they have left over after they've taken care of everything else. They are telling us what their priorities are – that their faith is a luxury to be indulged only after the "necessities" are looked after. It usually means a severe case of spiritual poverty, and that the church is not one of their priorities. As the old saying goes, "actions speak louder than words."

People who make a pledge take their giving, their commitment, more seriously. The proportion of their income that pledgers give is about three times that offered by people who simply toss their spare cash into the plate on Sunday morning.

Envelopes

In order to keep track of who gives what so that income tax receipts can be sent out at the end of the year, most congregations provide envelopes.

These envelopes also make it possible for you and me to tell our church how much of our offering should be used locally and how much should go to outreach (the Mission and Service Fund), or to other special appeals.

Some congregations budget a certain amount for Mission and Service and if not enough designated money comes in they'll make up the difference from regular funds. Others just send whatever comes in on the plates.

I was born in the 1930s when we used cash – nickels, dimes, and dollar bills – for everything we bought. Hardly anything

was bought on credit. If you didn't have the money, you started saving, or you did without. Money was something you could touch and feel and smell.

In the 1960s, most of us had bank accounts, and we began to use cheques more and more. A cheque was as good as cash. Well, almost. Then in the 1970s along came credit cards, and our use of money became even less personal. We didn't pay for things we bought – we paid the credit card company.

In the late 1980s and early 1990s, automatic debit cards came along. We began banking by telephone or computer. Now, the cash I carry in my wallet is for small stuff. Incidentals.

The important stuff is all done by postdated cheques, credit or debit cards, or automatic deductions. If I put cash on the plate on Sunday, I begin to think of the church as just one of those incidentals I pay for with cash. My church becomes a low-priority item.

Up to PAR

That's why most churches have available a Pre-Authorized Remittance plan. PAR for short. Bev and I use postdated cheques, but we could also use PAR. Some congregations supply you with a little card you can put on the offering plate when it comes around. It says you've been using PAR.

I find it kind of funny. In our congregation, the folks who give the most to the church are the ones who don't put any money on the offering plate when it goes by. They use PAR or postdated cheques.

In some congregations, they don't pass the plate at all. They have a contribution box at the entrance where people put their envelopes or cash. That's because some people feel embarrassed about passing the plate without putting something on it.

Strangely, using those offering boxes doesn't seem to have

186

reduced the contributions to the church. However, sometimes there isn't as much loose cash given.

The important thing in all this is our attitude. With PAR, our church giving is up there with the other highly important things in our life.

How it all adds up

When you put them all together, the statistics are interesting. In 2014, the people of the United Church gave almost $250 million. Of that, just a bit more than $27 million went to the national church.

That sounds like a lot of bucks until you realize that the United Church is a big denomination. Next to the Roman Catholic Church, it's probably the biggest non-profit organization in Canada, with branches in just about every town (though fewer in Quebec). It's bigger than all the service clubs put together.

Our giving in the United Church has been going up, bit by bit, but it hasn't even kept up with inflation. People are giving a smaller percentage of their income, and the church is winding up with less buying power.

Spending the money

The largest slice of the money we send to the national church goes to a variety of causes and projects across Canada and in many developing countries. This includes various kinds of social service and social action ministries, education, evangelism and leadership development. Some of it is used to support small congregations that wouldn't be able to stand on their feet otherwise.

Then, of course, there's administration. So far, the United Church has a good record of spending less than most non-profit

organizations to keep the wheels turning. If you want more specific numbers about any of the above, search the United Church website for "Audited Financial Statement." It's all there. No secrets.

When you don't agree

A major problem with democracies like the United Church is that there is no way to please everybody. No matter what a church this size does (or doesn't do), somebody is going to be upset. And because the church is doing so many things, all of us can find something that'll tie our shirt into knots.

"How can I give money to something I disagree with?" There are people who have stopped giving to the church because they didn't like what it has said about racism or sexuality or something else.

"How can I give money to something I disagree with?" is a good question if you've taken a careful look at the subject and have studied the facts. It's not a good question if all you know is what you've read in the papers or heard on the radio or seen on the Internet.

If you've checked out the facts and still disagree with the church's actions, then you should be speaking out in your congregation and at presbytery. To simply grumble to yourself and a few friends, then quit, is a cheap cop-out.

On the other hand, maybe you've done all you can to change things. You feel, as a matter of conscience, that you simply can't support a certain thing the church is doing. Then you should send your donation to the United Church office in Toronto with a covering letter that tells the people there how you'd like your money used.

If you disagree with everything the United Church does, you're in the wrong denomination.

A lack of connection

One of the hardest things for an organization like the United Church to do is to keep us all feeling connected with the outreach work that our givings go to. The stewardship people in the national office try valiantly to keep that connection warm.

In most congregations, we have a "Minute for Mission" every Sunday that tells us about a project or venture or a need that our money goes toward. And there's lots of other information available in every congregation, for example in *Mandate* magazine.

The reality is that many folks want to control where their money goes. And so the national church becomes weaker as more and more money is kept in the local congregations.

In the long run, I think the congregations themselves will suffer most. And so will individual givers. When we focus our energies and money only on ourselves, our view of the world gets narrow and ingrown. And somehow, our spirit shrinks in the process.

Changing attitudes

The people who benefit most from the giving are the givers. We give, first of all, because we need to give. It does us good. It helps us grow. Giving helps us get our perspective straight and our priorities in order. And it becomes a practical statement of what we really believe.

We need to give in the same way that we need to be in a caring relationship with other people. The other day Bev woke up with her arthritis bothering her because it was raining and the clouds were down near our eyebrows. On the way home from an errand, I bought a large flowering plant. She was delighted and I got a big hug. We give because our love needs to be expressed.

That's why we give our money as a part of our worship. The offering in church is an act of worship, an expression of our love of God, just like communion or prayer. We feel so strongly about money because it is such a powerful symbol of our self-worth. That's why giving our money to God, as an act of worship, is so important. It's a way of giving ourselves to God.

The second reason for giving is that the church needs the money for the work in our own congregation and community, as well as in the work of the whole church around the world.

Making our money work for us

The United Church, for the most part, handles its money well. In overseas work and here at home, it generally makes a dollar do more than most other organizations, religious or secular. That's because so much is done by volunteers.

I feel, personally, that we're much too timid about the way we raise money in our congregations. Too often, we pussyfoot around, afraid of offending someone and losing their buck a week.

We need to bluntly remind people that what they do with their money is a statement of their faith. If I just put a toonie a week on the plate that would represent about .02 percent of my income. I sometimes wonder if God feels offended or hurt by such paltry giving.

Which brings us to that word "stewardship" again. The best definition I've heard so far is, "Stewardship is what you do after you say, 'I believe.'"

Or, to quote Jesus again, "Where your treasure is, there your heart will be also."

10

This We Believe

You shall love the Lord your God with all your heart,
and with all your soul, and with all your strength, and
with all your mind; and your neighbour as yourself.
Luke 10:27

You can't get very far talking
about a church unless you talk about what people in that church
believe.

But first I need to repeat something I said right at the beginning. What follows is my own personal perspective. Each person's beliefs – their spirituality – is as unique as a fingerprint. That's true of all people, everywhere. What's different about the United Church (as well as a number of other faith groups) is that we think this is not only okay, but one of our great assets.

One of the reasons I joined the United Church is because nobody tried to hammer my ideas into a particular slot or shape. This chapter, or for that matter any part of the book, tells you

where my thinking and feeling is, at this point in my life. It's not any kind of official statement.

One of the things I believe is that God made each of us unique, so that we can experience the holy in our own special way and share that with others. We learn more from the folk we disagree with than we do from those who agree with everything we say. So I don't expect you or anyone else to agree with everything that follows. In fact, if you do, you're probably not paying much attention.

There's a huge spectrum of folks in the United Church – possibly a wider spectrum than in most other denominations. We have folks on the far left who claim to be essentially atheist, to folks on the far right who would like us to read the Bible literally. Holding that spectrum of beliefs in a creative tension is our greatest blessing and our most difficult challenge. And people do drop off on both those edges.

Song of Faith

I've found myself inspired by a document – no, call it a poem or a song – which I found on the national United Church website. You can find it by searching for "A Song of Faith."

Read it all the way through. It will give you a very good sense of what the United Church of Canada is about.

Spiritual food

I think about the wide variety of ways in which people work out their spirituality, somewhat in the way that I think about food.

Each person has their own likes and dislikes when it comes to food, and their own ways of preparing it. Even within one family. I love peanut butter. Bev barely tolerates it. We've enjoyed being invited to friends' homes and sharing the food they

prepare. Similar to what we do, but different. And then there are foods that come from other cultures and traditions. I'm particularly fond of Japanese food. My tastes in food were developed because of what I ate as a child, but, as an adult, I've experienced the delight of many different food traditions. All of it is good food.

In much the same way, there are many kinds of spirituality, and what feels most comfortable to me was probably conditioned largely by what I experienced as a child. As an adult, I've broadened my view to appreciate the spirituality of many different traditions and people. Learning from them, I enrich my own sense of the presence of God.

When it comes to food, you can have a healthy, nutritious diet using many different kinds of ingredients from many different sources. But, of course, some foods are more nutritious than others, and there's all kinds of junk food being waved under our noses. Junk food is full of empty calories and fills you up, but weakens your body in the process and leaves you vulnerable to a variety of illnesses.

In the same way, all kinds of spiritual junk food is waved under our noses. Much of it comes in the consumerism promoted by very clever advertising that tells us that we can satisfy our deepest needs in the shopping mall. Spiritual junk food might fill us up for a while, but leaves us vulnerable to diseases like loneliness and depression.

Theology is fun

Theology is to religion what recipe books and nutritional guides are to food. It's a way of talking about things we believe about ourselves and about God. So here we go. I'll try to go straight down the middle, which probably means that I'll have both sides mad at me. So be it.

Theology is simply thinking or talking about God or any question of faith. When people talk about their own spirituality, they are talking theology.

Theology doesn't have to be complicated or academic or dry. It's about everyday life. It's about what we think is most important. And it isn't half as mysterious as many people think.

Most of what I know about theology has come from sitting in the pew on Sunday mornings and then trying to apply what I hear and feel to my work and home life. I have found some good books that have helped me grow in my faith, some of which are listed at the back of this one, on page 260.

I have had lots of lively and fun discussions with friends over the years, in study groups and over coffee. That's the kind of learning I've always liked best. I don't have a university degree in theology and I'm not an ordained minister.

I discovered along the way that, as long as I relax, I can take the subject seriously without taking myself and my own opinions too seriously. When I do that, talking and studying theology is fun!

Building a personal faith

Working out your own faith is a bit like building a house. You need a good solid foundation and structure. You need a roof that doesn't leak. If you've got that, you can redecorate, even move walls around, without having the house tumble down around your ears.

I remember seeing a house in rural Ontario a few years ago. There was a rickety centre section to which one lean-to after another had been added over the years. Some people's faith (their theology) is like that house – a series of lean-tos. One afterthought leaning against another and a few isolated ideas not attached to anything. Not a good place to live and not a faith that's going to work for you.

194

A personal faith has to be more than an idea from here, a scripture verse or two from there, and a few wise old sayings. What we say about one part of our faith should make sense in terms of the other parts. I don't mean that everything has to be logical. But we need to have a sense that the things we believe fit together into a whole. Otherwise it's hard to live that faith.

Our personal faith, our spirituality, needs to work for us in good times and in bad. A few of my friends have put together a personal spirituality that seems to be very thin. They don't notice all the beauty – the daily blessings that happen all around them – and when something bad happens, they blame it on God. "A loving God wouldn't let this happen…"

Their "do-it-yourself" faith didn't seem to help them much when pain and tragedy came along. A personal faith needs to stand the test of tragedy, as Bev and I found ours did when our son died. A "feel-good" spirituality is not robust enough to handle some of the struggles that come with life.

My statement doesn't cover the waterfront. There's plenty more I could say about any one of these subjects. After the first edition of this book was published, people kept asking me to expand on this chapter.

So I did. If you want an expanded version of what follows, I have written a book called *God for Beginners*, which you can order from the Wood Lake Publications website or from Amazon.

God

As a Christian, the best way for me to learn what God is like is to study the life of Jesus. By what Jesus was, what he said and did, and in the way he died and overcame death, we see a clearer picture of God.

But people were thinking and learning about God long before the time of Jesus. Thousands of years earlier, a couple

named Abraham and Sarah set out on a pilgrimage. They were led by a God who seemed to have chosen them to get something important started.

The children of Abraham and Sarah seemed like such an unimportant little band of people; always being whacked by more powerful nations. But these people, Hebrews they called themselves, had a God who seemed to stick with them, a God who heard their cry and brought them out of slavery in Egypt and into a promised land.

They called this God "Yahweh." Through Moses, they were given a series of commandments and, through the prophets that followed, the Hebrew people repeatedly heard Yahweh say, "I will be your God and you shall be my people."

For the Hebrews, this was a covenant – permanent and binding on both sides. Over the centuries, they came to four very important conclusions about God.

First, the Hebrews realized that there was only one God and that was Yahweh.

Second, they learned that Yahweh was just. This God wasn't like some of the kings and despots they saw around them who would play favourites and bend rules. What God said, God meant.

Third, they learned that God was good. God wanted the best for them as a nation. They even began to suspect that God actually loved them, though they weren't sure what that meant.

Fourth, they discovered that the covenant was not with individuals, but with the whole people. They were all in it together. What one of them did affected all of them. Furthermore, God spoke to them, usually through the prophets, as a people, not as individuals.

That's the basic story told in the Hebrew scriptures, or to use the more traditional term, the Old Testament. Now we get

to the part traditionally called the New Testament, but which I prefer to call the Christian scriptures.

Jesus

During much of the time that's covered in those Old Testament stories, the prophets had been hinting, sometimes even predicting, the coming of a Messiah. This would be someone who could save the Hebrew people from their enemies and offer them new hope.

Many people expected a Messiah who would look like Ulysses and would sweep across the nation and kick out the hated Romans, who occupied their country.

Well, the Messiah did come. As promised, but not as expected. Mary was a young country girl. Joseph was the village carpenter. When Mary was gloriously pregnant, they took a trip to Bethlehem to be counted in a census. We know the rest of the story. Or, we think we do.

In misery and pain

A number of years ago I visited a cave-like stable in a Lebanese village. The professor who showed it to me said it probably was very similar to the stable in which Jesus was born.

It was stinking dirty. Rats and cockroaches scurried away as we walked in. The animals were scrawny and mangy. It didn't look a bit like our Christmas card pictures.

Then I thought about Mary, really just a girl, giving birth to her first child in that stinking stable. There might have been a midwife, but the story doesn't mention one. Certainly, she was without modern medical help. I thought about that and the image of Jesus on the cross came to mind. I realized that Jesus came into the world the same way he left – in misery and pain.

Human and divine

When God became human in Jesus of Nazareth, there was no holding back. Jesus wasn't half-God, half-human. Jesus was completely both. On the human side, Jesus had every potential weakness, every problem, every passion that we have. God didn't fake it. Jesus was not walking around pretending to be human.

In the person of Jesus, God lived with a body like mine, lived with fears and fantasies the way I do, knew the joy of one moment and the horror of the next, ran into trouble with the authorities, was teased and taunted and made to look like a fool and was finally hung up like a common crook. So God knows what it's like to be human. To be one of us. That's very important to me.

Jesus also knew what it was like to be God. He was able to say, "The Father and I are one," which meant he was both completely human and completely God at the same time. It's one of those things we puzzle over. A paradox. Our experience tells us it's true, even though our minds complain that it doesn't make sense. Jesus with us as both human and God. It's what we call "incarnation."

When Jesus was about 30, he began a ministry that was to change the world. He gathered a small group of disciples (or followers or pupils) around him and spent hours and days teaching them. When crowds gathered, he told stories. We call them parables.

These parables were far more than cute stories to illustrate a point. Jesus used them to push people to the edge of their understanding. They always felt they understood, but never completely. And each time they heard or read the parable again, they found new truth there.

That, by the way, is one of the reasons we keep reading the same scriptures over and over.

A complex person

The crowds often gathered around Jesus because of reports about what he did – healing cripples, curing the blind, feeding thousands with just a little food. But they stayed to listen because he spoke with authority in words they could understand. Even so, sometimes they just didn't get it. But they got enough to make them want more – to make them want to grow.

Jesus was a complex person. He was different things to different people. That's why there are four different accounts of his life, death, and resurrection, each one seeing Jesus from a different perspective. Those are the four gospels – Matthew, Mark, Luke, and John that you find in the Bible – all of them written quite a while after Jesus died.

When Jesus was dying on the cross, he found himself totally alone, totally separated from God. When he hung there on that cross, the agony shuddered through his body. Abandoned by his best friends and feeling abandoned by God, he yelled, "My God, my God, why have you forsaken me?" He was yelling for all of us, who are caught in the hell of separation from God. Caught in living death.

It was real pain. Real fear. Real anger. Jesus was abandoned by his friends. And he certainly felt forsaken by God. He died the way he was born – in screaming, bloody pain.

Jesus didn't die as some sort of prepayment. Nor did he die to "pay" for our sins. I can't go out and be as rotten as I want, as some might suggest we should do, because my sins are paid for in advance. Jesus died because he confronted the religious and political establishment. He was accused of treason and executed. It's not something God arranged in advance.

But as we allow ourselves to think about and feel the pain of his dying, we can experience with him the full impact of human sin. It showed us graphically how the lust for power,

greed, ignorance, selfishness, and status can destroy what is best and finest about God's creation. Jesus' willingness to die showed us how far the power of love can take us.

On the surface, it sounds as if the story of Jesus comes to a very tragic end. He was executed out on the edge of town where thousands of people had been crucified before him. Not what you'd call a great finish for a Messiah.

Except it wasn't the finish. It was the beginning. Soon, there were whispers going around; people claiming he was alive. Others yelled, "Hogwash!" But the stories kept right on. So did the arguments.

He had been put in a borrowed tomb. A huge stone was rolled in front so nobody could steal the body.

But, somehow, the stone was rolled away and the body was gone.

People still argue about what really happened. And what it all meant. In the end, it's not really important. You see, it's not the absence of his corpse from an empty tomb that convinces us. It's his presence in our empty lives!

The Resurrection

The opposite of death is life. The opposite of sin is love. The opposite of despair is hope. Often, the pain on one side may be the beginning of joy on the other.

That's why we call the Friday Jesus gasped out his last breath, Good Friday. We call it "good" because it made Easter possible.

Separation, death, and despair are never the final answer in God's way of doing things. God's love is the ultimate power. It is the power that overcomes the sin of alienation – the sin that crucified Jesus on the cross. At Easter, we celebrate the triumph of life over death. In our churches you'll see an empty cross. Jesus isn't hanging there anymore.

Love was the final word that burst upon the pages of history when Jesus came back from the dead, as if God was saying, "You can't keep me down. You can't get rid of me. Try your worst, but I will still be here with you, always. I'm not going away, and I will always love you."

One of the pictures you often see in our churches was drawn by United Church artist Willis Wheatley. It's a drawing of Jesus laughing, which he called "Jesus Christ – Liberator." It's the laughter of togetherness. Jesus laughs with us in the love that liberates us from the icy power of alienation.

That's why we sometimes call ourselves an "Easter People." We're a people of the Resurrection. We can celebrate a deep-down joy, even when we're so low it's hard to know which way is up.

The birthday of our church

Before Jesus died, he told the disciples he wouldn't leave them. After he died, they had, for a short while, the joy of the Resurrection. But then he was gone again. The disciples wandered around disorganized and confused, not sure what to do.

They gathered for the annual harvest feast, though it almost seemed more like a meeting of a memorial society.

Suddenly, something happened. The disciples described it later as the sound of rushing wind. Tongues of fire danced among them. They began to speak in strange languages, yet the people who gathered around understood.

Some said the disciples were drunk, but one of the disciples, a wiry fisherman named Peter, gave what turned out to be the first sermon of the Christian church. Looking back on it later, they knew it was the day the church was born. We have celebrated that birthday ever since as Pentecost, which many churches symbolize by using the colour red. One year the chil-

dren in our church sang, "Happy Birthday to Us."

The tiny band of disciples, hurt and confused because their leader was gone, became filled with power and possibilities. They called it the Holy Spirit. From that beginning, the Christian faith spread literally all over the world. Now there probably isn't a single country anywhere that hasn't got a Christian church of some kind. Even Antarctica.

Why a church?

Many people wonder if we really need a church in which to express our faith. Do we need all that organization, that institution, all that tradition, all the stuff that goes with a church?

I can only speak for myself. I tried to take a "distance education" course once. "I don't need classes and cranky instructors and all that stuff," I told myself. "I can work on my own!"

Except I didn't. After an enthusiastic start, it dropped off. The plain truth is that I need others to help me get where I want to go. I can't make it on my own.

I also need a way of thinking about my faith, a way to talk about it, a way to express it. A few years ago, I heard some lectures by Rabbi Wosk of Vancouver. I asked him why Jews need all the stuff that is called the Torah – all the structure and background and rules and traditions.

The Rabbi took the glass of water from his speaker's stand. He poured some of it on the floor. "The water on the floor is the same stuff as the water in the glass. But to drink it, I need it in the glass."

In other words, the church – its traditions and community – provide the container, the structure, through which we can experience our faith. And yes, of course there are many different kinds of "containers."

Learning from others

That's why United Church people are borrowing from some other faith traditions – drinking from other cups, if you like.

The idea of "spiritual directors" – people trained to help us walk and grow in our faith journey – came to us from our Roman Catholic friends, who sometimes draw on earlier, deeper wells of faith. Now spiritual direction is a growing movement in the United Church.

We've also tried to pick out the useful parts from other forms of spirituality, both old and new. Looking back into our ancient roots, we discover gifts like Christian meditation, healing touch, prayer groups, and contemplative prayer. And we're learning lots from non-Christian forms of spirituality.

Our eyes have been opened by the Truth and Reconciliation Commission, and by many First Nations individuals, to the rich and varied heritage they bring to our country and our church. They often have a strong tradition of meditation and spirituality. They understand the power of ceremonies. Gradually they are teaching us. We've been much too slow in learning from them.

I have a nephew, a yoga teacher, who has taught me much about the Buddhist practice of mindfulness. Some of us are rediscovering the power of submission to God's love from Muslim practices. And, of course, we are digging deep into our own Christian traditions to find the treasure hidden there.

Let's be clear what we're talking about. Spirituality is a very quiet thing. You don't know it's there until you stand close to someone who has allowed their spirituality to grow.

Some express it by holding their hands up and by the way they speak. For most, though, it's a very quiet, subtle thing. One church leader described the spirituality of a person he had met in an inner-city congregation: "Somehow, when you were

with her, you just wanted to be a better person."

A deep spirituality is the greatest gift we can receive as we live and grow in the church. It's not something foreign that we import. It is there, inside each one of us, waiting like a seed in springtime to grow and blossom. Those seeds grow in a garden called the church. A garden is successful only when the plants within it are vigorous and strong.

I'm convinced that The United Church of Canada will survive and even thrive because many of its people are developing a strong, lively, spirituality.

Three in one

Christians have three ways of describing God. We call that the Holy Trinity. The word Trinity isn't mentioned in the Bible, but the three ways of understanding God certainly are. The concept of the Trinity evolved later, as a way of describing what people found as they read their Bibles and experienced God's presence.

We think of Yahweh, the God of our ancestors, as all-powerful, everlasting, all-holy, all-loving. God as Creator! Eventually, we simply run out of superlatives, because there's nothing we can ever say about God and respect for creation that would do justice to the reality.

Traditionally, when we think of that all-powerful, creator God, we have used the word "Father." Nothing wrong with that, except it's too limiting. I find it much easier to think of God as Mother, possibly because I was much closer to my own mother than to my father. But categories like male and female don't apply. God is not a human, although we often use human metaphors to think and talk about God.

Many people find it helpful to think of God as a parent, a strong, just, and loving mother or father. Of course, if you have

not had a happy family life, that may not be a very helpful metaphor at all. You may then need to think of God as the very best aunt, or uncle, or friend or teacher or social worker you can imagine.

When we think about God who knows what it's like to be us, we think of Jesus – God the Son. One of the names for Jesus was "Emmanuel," which means, "God with us." So if we want a flesh and blood example of what God is like, we think of Jesus, the Christ.

Sometimes we're aware that God is right around us and inside us. That's when we speak of God as the Holy Spirit.

There aren't three Gods, just three different ways of knowing one God. There's the classic example of the shamrock leaf, which legend tells us St. Patrick used as way of describing the Trinity in Ireland. Three petals make up one leaf.

You can also think of it like a braid of hair. All the hair begins on the same head, but you can separate it into three strands that make up a braid. Every strand depends on the other two, and at the tip, they all come together again. Our joyful, lifelong journey is about getting to know the love of that God, who is known to us in so many ways, but most particularly through these three strands of spirituality we call the Holy Trinity.

Of course, there are far more than three ways of thinking about God. A Jewish friend recently gave me a list of 100 names for God. The Hindu tradition has 1,000 names for God (Lord Vishnu).

It doesn't matter much what you call God, but it *does* matter that you have an awareness of a God of love and justice active in your life.

Some people feel the traditional formula – Father, Son, and Holy Spirit – should be recast, and it often is in songs, prayers,

and sermons. We've kept it in the baptism service to keep our connection with other denominations, for whom this formula is fundamental.

Having said that, there are more and more Christians who have trouble accepting the whole idea of the Trinity. If it gives you trouble, lay it gently aside, because it has deep meaning for others. But don't just walk away. Work on your own way of thinking about God.

Revelation

God communicates with us in many ways. We call that communication "revelation." Some kinds of revelation are dramatic. Others are very ordinary. Slow, careful study is revelation. Day-by-day living is revelation.

God's most important communication came in the form of a human being when God said, "Look, I'll show you what I'm like." In Jesus, I see more clearly than anywhere else what the God we worship is really like.

God speaks to us through scriptures. The Bible tells a story of people struggling to know the will of God and of God struggling to get through to them. By reading that story, we can come to know God's dream for us and for the world.

Revelation may also come in a sudden insight, a gift of the Holy Spirit. It may follow months of wondering and puzzling, or it may come suddenly, as a surprise.

We can read and hear the story of "saints," people who have been open to what God is trying to tell them. Saints are simply ordinary people who have taken the time to listen, and who struggle hard to live their faith.

God speaks to us through our traditions. That includes our family traditions, such as how we celebrate a birthday. And it includes our church traditions. How we honour and mark the

seasons of our lives leads us to an understanding of what they mean. God is quite capable of communicating through a wide variety of traditions, of which the United Church tradition is only one.

Science and religion

God speaks to us through science and logic. There is no contradiction between science and religion, even though scientists and religious people have often argued. Something cannot be scientifically true if it is not also religiously true. If, for instance, you believe the theory of evolution from Monday through Friday, but on Sunday morning you believe that God created the world in seven days as it says in the book of Genesis, then something's haywire.

Much of the argument between scientists and religious people has been pretty silly. Scientists and religious people both make the mistake of thinking of the Bible as a historical or scientific document. It's neither. For instance, the first creation story (at the very beginning of the Bible) is a poem. The second one (about Adam and Eve and the snake) is a legend. Both writings contain deep truth, and together with scientific theories, help us understand who we are and why we are here. Both stories, like many others in the Bible, are simply making certain statements about faith, and about God's presence in the world.

It's the difference between "truth" and "fact." To say that the colours of the rainbow are caused by the refraction of light by droplets of water is a fact. To say that the rainbow is beautiful is truth. One does not contradict the other. Both help us understand rainbows. Science and religion are two different ways of shining light on the mystery of all that is. We need both.

Nature

Certainly, God communicates through nature. When Noah saw the rainbow, he understood it to be a symbol of God's promise. When I work in my garden, God speaks to me through the wonder of growing plants. Photographing tiny buds and flowers is my hobby. I see the creator God every time I press the shutter, and marvel at the scientific explanations of the miracle of growth and evolution.

I've heard people say, "I can worship God just as well on the golf course as I can in church." That may be true. But I've only met one person (clergy) who did. Most of us are so busy trying to stay out of the water hazard, the last thing we think about is God.

We can sense the presence of God as we stand on a mountain drinking in the view. We can sense the presence of God in the hospital as we hold the hand of a dying friend. We can sense the presence of God as we sing together in church, or in deep conversation with someone we love.

God isn't limited to any of those things. God may thump you or me on the head with a particular experience or speak to us through a moment of grief or pain or joy. God communicates in a billion and one different ways.

There is a book in the Bible called *Revelation*. It's a book written in a kind of code to a group of Christians caught in a particularly dangerous situation. Some people have used that book, quite irresponsibly, to predict things like the second coming of Christ and the end of the world.

That's pure fantasy and a convenient cop-out for people who are trying to run away from the realities of this present life. Some people find it easier to dream about "pie in the sky" than to respond creatively to a hurting world.

I can understand the temptation. But it doesn't work. Prob-

lems we avoid have a habit of blind-siding us when we least expect it.

Prayer

People experience God communicating with them in many different ways, but for many (perhaps most) it's through prayer. But prayer, like so many other things in the Christian faith, is hard to describe. It's something you understand only when you've experienced it.

When Bev was away at school before we were married, I wrote her letters almost every day. Now that we've been married for almost 60 years, we still need to keep communicating.

It's easier now that we are both retired, and we're in the same house together all day every day. Even so, when something serious comes up, we need to stop doing all the stuff that keeps us busy, and sit down together.

But when we were working, Bev and I sometimes felt like ships passing in the night, with no real communication happening. So we had a little ritual. Saturday mornings, before we got dressed or did anything else, we sat down for a long cup of coffee and just talked. We might talk about how to get a spot out of the rug, or about our kids, or about a problem in our marriage or about our faith.

For love to be born, and for love to grow, and for love to continue, there must be communication. In our relationship with God, prayer is that communication. Bev and I would lose our marriage if we didn't make a conscious effort to spend time with each other. In the same way, we can lose our faith if we don't make a conscious effort to spend time with God.

God is easy to talk with. God understands any language spoken by anybody – the simple words of a two-year-old, the complicated language of a professional theologian, or the coarse

language of a street person. In fact, prayer doesn't really need words at all.

Some people "can't think of anything to say," when they pray. They spend time in silence, just listening for whatever God has to tell them or show them. Silence is the language of God.

Prayer should never be forced. It is a natural thing to do, but it needs learning, like a child learning to walk or talk. It needs constant practice, like learning to play a musical instrument.

But even if you haven't prayed for a long time and you feel awkward and uncomfortable, your prayer is heard.

The Bible

The Bible is the world's most amazing book. There are three parts to it: the Hebrew scriptures, the Apocrypha, and the Christian scriptures. The Apocrypha is usually included in Bibles used in the Anglican and Roman Catholic traditions. The rest of us, including the United Church, use the other two portions, although occasionally a few of us are beginning to discover treasures in the Apocrypha.

The Hebrew scriptures (or the Old Testament) began as stories told around campfires by scraggly shepherds, as songs sung on lonely hillsides, and as rules and records and regulations written down by a few scribes.

Gradually, some of the stories, writings, and songs began to have more authority than others, as people agreed, "God speaks to us through this."

The Christian scriptures (or the New Testament) had similar beginnings, but came together during a much shorter time. After that first Easter, the disciples expected Jesus to return very soon. So they didn't bother to write things down. They simply told and retold the stories of what Jesus had said and done.

As time went by and as some of the original witnesses died off, the first Christians started to write things down so that more people might know the story of Jesus and the early church.

There were many stories about Jesus written down, and various letters and papers by early church leaders were collected. Not all the stories agreed with each other. It didn't matter. Each of those writings had something important in them. But it wasn't until about 300 years after Jesus that the Bible, as we know it today, was decided upon.

Proof texts

The Bible is often abused. People go to it for a phrase here or a sentence there to support a favourite idea. The Bible is such a rich mine of experiences that you can find material there that, when used the wrong way, will support just about anything.

That's one of the reasons we have such a variety of denominations and religious groups. Each claims to have founded its faith on the Bible. Each group (including those of us in the United Church) can easily find things in scripture that seem to support what we believe.

Then how does anyone know which interpretation is right? There's no easy answer to that, but there are a few clues.

If you went into the forest near my home and walked up to one of the trees, you might say, "Aha! This is a birch tree. Therefore, this is a birch forest."

You would be wrong. It's a pine forest with a few birch trees in it. To see what the forest is like, you need to back away and take a broad look at the whole thing. From a mountaintop or an airplane.

Similarly, when you want to know what the Bible is saying, you've got to look at the whole book. Only by understanding the Bible's whole context can you decide how to interpret any part of it.

Here's another clue. I've been asked, from time to time, "Do you believe in the Bible?"

My answer is, "No, I believe in the God the Bible shows me, especially through the life and teachings of Jesus, the Messiah."

If the whole purpose of the Bible is to point to the Messiah, then everything in it should be understood in terms of that Messiah. So whenever we read something in the Bible, we need to ask, "How does this tally with who Jesus Christ was; with what he said and did?"

Because we are individuals, each of us reads the Bible in a slightly different way. When we listen to what others have found there, we broaden and deepen our own understanding.

A final clue. The church is there to help us. We can check our understanding against what the church internationally and through the ages has understood.

We're not in this by ourselves. None of us is as smart as all of us. Listening to others' insights helps us understand our own. Conversations with friends, informally or in study groups, is one of the most important things that happens in church.

Let the stories speak

It is important to remember that the Bible is not primarily a book of history or a book of rules or a book of preaching, though you'll find all of those in the Bible. It is definitely not science.

People in biblical times often told stories to communicate their faith. Some of those stories were historical and some were not. Many are legends that contain powerful ideas and profound truth. Some parts have no particular significance at all, religious or otherwise. I wonder how they got into the Bible.

It's important not to get caught up in arguments about how much of the Bible is historically accurate, and how much is not. That's an interesting discussion, but it's not the main show.

First, let the stories speak to you. They can fill your spirit and speak the truth, whether they are historically accurate or not. When you've fallen in love with this marvellous book – when you have learned how it can feed your soul – then you might want to listen to what the scholars are saying about how much of the Bible is historical.

It's a bit like a good meal. The food is delicious, so you enjoy it and you let it provide strength and nourishment for your body. That's the main thing. Later you may ask the host for the recipe, but that comes after you've enjoyed the food.

You can starve to death if all you do is collect and analyze recipes.

Born again

We hear the phrase "born again" used even in ways that have nothing to do with religion. The phrase comes from the gospel of John where Jesus is talking to an important leader named Nicodemus. It's the only place Jesus uses those words.

I think he was trying to tell Nicodemus that believing meant more than changing the surface of things. It meant turning your personal world upside down and inside out. It meant changing your whole outlook on life, your reasons for doing things and, most of all, your relationship to God. It meant starting all over.

It's possible to be "born again" in many ways. It may come as a flash of love and joy so powerful you never forget the moment. It can also happen slowly, over a long period of painful searching. Either way, it changes your life. Dramatically.

Some people say they have been "born again," but their emotional high doesn't change the way they handle money, how they vote, or how they relate to the poor and underprivileged here and in other countries. It makes no difference to the way they live or how they think.

It's a little like the old Plymouth I used to drive. The odometer went all the way up to 99,999, then back to zero. "I have a born-again car," I told my friends. But it was still the same car with all the same squeaks, rattles, and problems. Nothing had really changed.

The danger is that a born-again experience may simply inoculate us against the real thing. One strong emotional experience doesn't make a life. Christian faith is like being in love with another person. You can say, "I love you," and have a deep experience of love and commitment. But that love and commitment must be lived every single day. As soon as we stop living our love, it begins to die.

Another word we often use for being born again, a better one actually, is "conversion." People change from one way of seeing life to another. The way we think, act, and live changes. Our values are converted. Many of us find that conversion is an ongoing process as we discover new areas of our life that need God's love.

The rules

One of God's gifts to the Hebrew people was the "Law." Much of the Hebrew scriptures is about God's law and our response to it. The law was both an overall principle by which to live and a series of "rules and regulations." Those laws were continually refined and simplified.

One great summary was the Ten Commandments. Another was quoted by Jesus as two commandments – to love God and to love your neighbour as yourself. In the end, Jesus condensed all laws into one. "Love one another as I have loved you."

Laws are important. We need them to set the boundaries of behaviour when some people aren't willing to live by love. But laws also tend to be rigid. They don't take into account all the

unusual circumstances in which people find themselves. It's easy to use the law, or "moral absolutes," to control people and to make them over according to your own biases.

Still, laws are useful and important. In our family, we always had rules about things like bedtime, behaviour, meals, and so on. But there were also times when we set aside those rules. There was a more important consideration.

Jesus tells us that rules are there to be used and obeyed, but love is a more important consideration. It's so easy to become lawyers when God wants us to be lovers.

Sin

There's a popular concept of sin. It's reflected in a wall plaque that reads, "Everything I like is indecent, immoral, or fattening."

Under that concept, sin is a collection of nasties like smoking, drinking, gambling, sex, or using naughty four-letter words. When those things are destructive to people, they are sinful. So are things like greed, pettiness, backbiting, pride, envy, and refusing to see our part in the sin of other people.

These sins are all symptoms of a more basic disease called "sinfulness." It is the disease of separation from God's love. We are always "living in sin" because, one way or another, we are always running away from God.

When Bev and I have a battle over something, one of us eventually has to swallow our pride and say, "Hey, I'm sorry." Until that happens, we both feel rotten. We both hurt because we are separated from each other. It's far worse when we're separated from God.

The problem is that our separateness from God is built-in. Our basic selfishness seems to be there the moment we're born. That's what theologians have sometimes called "original sin." Bridging that gap is what the journey of faith is all about. It

does not mean that we are "born bad."

A concept I like much better is called "original blessing." We are created, as the Bible says, "in the image of God." In some essential, fundamental ways, we are God-like.

Or as someone once said, "God don't make junk."

Justice

But there's a deeper and more difficult condition of sinfulness that we all live in. It is the systemic sin that is built into our social, economic, and political structures. It is a sin that has children starving in Africa, and people sleeping beside dumpsters a few blocks from where I live. It is a sin that denies dignity and acceptance to people because of the way God made them.

We can blame that on politicians and bank managers and military generals and assorted bigots and religious fundamentalists. But we all share the blame. So I think we are all called to act and vote and manage our lives and our finances in ways that help address that systemic sin.

The hardest thing to do is see our own sin. Especially the way we unthinkingly go along with sinful economic structures that keep people down.

It's far more fun to spot sin in other people. That's especially true of the sin of arrogance. We assume we know better than others "who are not as far along on their journey," or "who are not as liberated," or "who have not yet come to know Jesus." We Christians have a particular fondness for this sin. We tend to see the arrogance in everyone except ourselves.

Confession

"The harder I tries the behinder I gets." I saw that as a bumper sticker once and liked it. Sometimes I feel as if that applies to

my moral life, too. I really would like to have my life all together, to do all the right things at the right time, etc., etc. But, as some other wag said, "After I got it all together, I forgot where I put it."

Paul, in the Bible, had the same problem. "I want to do good, but I don't. I don't want to do bad, but I do. There's no help for me."

We keep screwing up. We are people. People screw up. That's why there are erasers on pencils.

We keep having to say, "I'm sorry," especially to the people we love. Especially to the God we love. In the church, we call that "confession."

Over and over, we need to tell God we're sorry. And it helps us to grow if we tell God very specifically what we're sorry about.

In the United Church, we confess our sins directly to God. We do that in prayer at home, at church, or anywhere. Sometimes we should also talk things over with another person. It really helps to tell another person what's bothering us. Often that other person can help us forgive ourselves and accept God's forgiveness.

Grace

Over my desk I have a quote attributed (out of context) to Martin Luther, the German reformer who kick-started the Protestant Reformation in the 16th century. "Sin boldly."

Luther isn't telling me to go and do all sorts of rotten things. He's telling me to recognize the fact that I am going to mess up. That's a given. So I shouldn't go walking on eggshells, trying desperately to stay out of trouble. "Live your life creatively and boldly," he seems to be saying, "and when you find you've done stupid things or even been profoundly cruel and unjust, know that God's grace is there for you."

Fix as much of the mess as you can. Make it up to people you have hurt. Reorganize your life so you don't keep doing cruel or stupid things over and over. But before and after and through it all, God loves you. Whether you know it or believe it or not. It's called grace.

Grace is a key Christian concept. Grace is God's love for us, regardless of what we might do. So we're called to love God and to love our neighbour, and to work for truth and justice. When we fall flat on our faces, God's love is there to help us to our feet again.

Forgiveness

When we say to someone, "Please forgive me!" they usually want to do that. But human patience wears thin if we keep screwing up over and over.

Not God's patience, though. God seems ready to forgive over and over and over, long past anything we humans can imagine.

Sometimes it seems as if God doesn't have any standards. No pride. God can get angry, but doesn't seem to stay angry. We do our worst, but as soon as we make the first tiny step back toward God's love, there it is.

The amazing thing about this love, this grace, is that we can never earn it. We can do things that will damage the love we have for each other. And we can do things that will violate our love for God. But we can never earn that love in the first place. That's part of that whole idea of "covenant." God has decided to love us, whether we deserve it or not, whether we love back or not.

When we are loved by another person, that love is the most precious gift they can give. When we are loved by God, it is the ultimate gift. And that love gives us our worth, our "justifica-

tion" as the theologians call it. That love means we're precious to God. What more do we need?

Heaven

I remember another journey of faith from many years ago when I was a boy about eight years old. The Second World War was raging. My dad had gone to Ottawa to work in the war effort. A few months later, we were to follow him, moving from our tiny hamlet of Horndean in southern Manitoba.

We went by train. Two days and two nights. I was terrified. As the train jerked forward to begin the journey, I remember crying in fear of the unknown in that big, mysterious city. I had never been to a city.

My mother put her arm around me. She held me very closely and said, "I'll be with you all the way, Ralph. All the way. And Dad will be waiting for us at the station when we get to Ottawa."

It was enough. I was still afraid, but no longer terrified. And now, as I face the very high probability of death in the next ten years (I'm 82), that memory has come back to offer its strength to me.

I don't know what lies beyond the mystery of death. No one does. But I face my own death, not without some fear, but very much aware of the strong arm of my mother-father God around me saying, "I'll be with you all the way, Ralph."

And it is enough.

Growing in faith

In a darkened basement, a single match can mean hope until, with that match, we find a candle to light. With the light from that candle, we find the fuse box and, with the electric light, we find the door leading to the sunlight. Each light dazzled our

eyes until we found a greater light that made the previous one seem so small by comparison.

Our growth in faith is like that. Each new experience, each new learning, makes earlier ones seem insignificant. The important thing, of course, isn't which light we're using now, but whether we keep on searching for a greater one.

The Christian faith is not something you arrive at. It's something you grow in. It's a process. A pathway. A journey. We often call ourselves pilgrims. The first Christians called themselves people of "The Way."

We're on our way together, and we know we're headed in the right direction. Even when we take a few too many detours.

We know we're on the right road because it's been marked by others who have gone before us. And we have the sure light of the whole Bible to see the pathway, and the company of fellow pilgrims called the church.

One of my favourite songs, and one we sing quite often in our church, is a South African Zulu folk song included in *Voices United*, "We are marching in the light of God!" Singing that song, standing beside my friends in the church, gives me strength to keep on my journey of faith.

But when all is said and done and we've fried our brains trying to understand the Christian faith, there is always more mystery. A mystery is not a puzzle we are trying to solve. Mystery is a well from which we draw life-giving water.

Wonderfully and mysteriously, the level of the water never goes down – the well of faith never runs dry.

11

Right, Wrong, and Maybe

In the beginning, God created the heaven and the earth…
So God created human beings in the divine image… and God
blessed them and said to them, "Be fruitful and multiply,
fill the earth and subdue it." So it was.
And God saw all creation, and it was very good.
Excerpts from Genesis 1 (paraphrased)

When you sing in the choir, you get to see things others miss. When Bev was the minister at Westbank United, I sang in the bass section. The choir pews were raised up so I got a good view of everything.

One Sunday, just as Bev was finishing her sermon, the door at the back opened tentatively. A man entered. I could see he was a bit unsteady on his feet. Iris, who always sat at the back of the church for just such situations, quickly found him a chair and invited him to sit. She whispered something into his ear, and he nodded.

Now it was time for communion. Along with a number of

others chosen to serve the communion that Sunday, Iris came up to the front. After the prayers and the invitation to everyone to "take and eat," Iris served the bread to the back rows, including our late visitor.

As she offered the plate of bread to him, he looked startled and in a loud voice said, "What the hell is this?" I couldn't hear her words, but Iris evidently explained it to his satisfaction. "Oh!" he said loudly.

Then the sacramental wine was served. (As in most United Churches, it was actually grape juice.) When Iris took the tray of glasses to the man in the back, he said loudly, "Good! I could use a drink." And so the service proceeded to its conclusion.

I saw the man again downstairs in the hall where we have coffee. My guess is that Iris invited him down for coffee and a sandwich. Around him, in quiet conversation, were several men who I knew were members of Alcoholics Anonymous. I went over to him to offer him my greetings. "You wouldn't want a drunk in this church," he said when I invited him to come back again. "Why not," said one of the men who was in AA. "You wouldn't be the only one."

I wish I could tell you a happy ending about the man finding a new direction for his life. He apparently came to an AA meeting at the church during the week, and he was back in church the following Sunday. Several of those AA men had tried to find out where he lived so they could keep in contact with him. He wouldn't tell them, and after the second Sunday he just disappeared.

The reason I'm telling you this story is because Iris and those men welcomed this person, even though he quite clearly was a little drunk and badly in need of clean clothes and a bath.

It was one of those moments when I found myself genuinely proud of my United Church. It's a story that illustrates in

a fundamental way how our concerns about hurting people are at the very heart of my denomination.

The two sides of morality

The story also illustrates what some would call a weakness, but which others see as a strength.

The United Church has been called "morally spineless" and "a church without standards." But others say it's simply taking Jesus seriously when he said, "The one of you who is faultless shall throw the first stone." Both sides have a point.

Most Christian churches believe that questions of right and wrong are central questions. As a society, we put maximum energy into questions like, "Does it work? Is it profitable? Is it legal?" But the church maintains that the central question must be, "Is it right? Does it serve the best interests of all of God's creation?"

When you think of it, that's about the only question left for humanity. With our technology developing so rapidly, "Will it work?" or "Is it possible?" can almost always be answered "Yes."

It certainly is possible for the nations of the world to spend billions of dollars a day on armaments (I'm not exaggerating!) while millions of people don't have adequate housing, education, or medical help.

But is it right?

Responses

There are at least three ways a church or an individual can respond to those kinds of questions. Two ways are easy. One is hard.

The "who cares?" way of decision-making is the easiest of all. You simply say, "Well, there's no way you can know what's right and wrong, so never mind. Do whatever feels good. And

smile!" You turn your decision-making over to the crowd you run with.

The "right's right!" method is a bit harder. You have to stand up for something. You say, "There's an absolute right and an absolute wrong to everything. For instance; divorce is wrong. Therefore, nobody gets a divorce. Period."

You turn your decision-making over to some "authority" who tells you exactly what those absolute rights and wrongs are. These "authorities" usually claim to know exactly how to interpret their "scripture," whether it's the Qur'an, the Communist Manifesto, capitalist Adam Smith's *The Wealth of Nations*, or the Bible.

It's tough

Then there's the "Jesus Way," and it's tough. It makes us think and choose. There's no United Church statement on how to make moral choices, but I think this third method would be endorsed by many in our denomination.

To understand this method, you have to look at the way Jesus decided what was right and wrong. Jesus had great respect for the Law, the rules by which the people of Israel tried to live. There's a story in the gospel of Luke about a wealthy man who came to Jesus and asked what he needed to do to have "eternal life." The first thing Jesus told him was to pay attention to the rules. He also told the man that there was much more to life than rules, but that was a good place to start.

On the other hand, when the lawyers of Jesus' time started getting picky about his friends eating corn on the Sabbath, Jesus didn't deny that they had broken Jewish law. He said, "The Sabbath is made for people. People were not made for the Sabbath." In other words, rules are there for your sake and mine. We're not here for the sake of the rules.

224

The gospels are peppered with stories of Jesus encountering people who had broken the law. He approached them all with love and understanding. Jesus' first concern always seemed to be for the people involved.

In the gospel of John, there's a story about a woman caught in adultery. In those days, sex with someone outside of marriage was a capital crime, though it was usually only the women who got punished for it. The woman in this story should have been executed by stoning, according to the law. A crowd of people standing around her had rocks in their hands.

Jesus was quick to see the sin of the folks with the rocks in their hands – the sin of pride and self-righteousness. So he said, "The one of you who is faultless shall throw the first stone." One by one they went sneaking off, knowing they were in no position to condemn the woman.

Jesus didn't say that what she had done was okay. But he didn't condemn her either. He said, "Go and sin no more."

What he did was the right thing for that woman in that situation at that time. The person was more important than the rules. But it is important to note that Jesus' concern was not only for the woman. It was also for the guys with the rocks in their hands.

Facing the hard questions

One of the hard moral questions is always, "What is the loving thing to do?" When my kids were small and ran out onto the street without looking, I scolded them. Sometimes I punished them. They didn't like it, but it was the loving thing to do.

Another central question is, "What will result in the greatest good for the greatest number of people involved?" In other words, justice with love. It can be a real dandy to sort out because sometimes the loving thing to do for the individual perpetuates the injustice for others.

The Bible indicates quite clearly that whenever somebody does something wrong, all of us are involved. As members of a society, we are part of the climate in which sin grows. So we need to ask God's forgiveness, while we do whatever we can to improve the climate.

As a church, we need to consider all these things when we work through various moral and ethical issues, which are almost never clear-cut. Then, as a church and as Christian individuals, we need to be a force for morality and justice in all aspects of society.

Choosing your battles

I find it really difficult sometimes. There are so many causes that need help, so many wrongs that need struggling against, so much justice to be struggled toward.

I don't know where to begin. I'd like to work towards a cleaner environment. I believe we need to do something about poverty, especially among women, children, and the elderly. I am keenly interested in international justice issues. On and on it goes. I feel burned out just thinking about all of it.

A few years ago, Clarke MacDonald, a former moderator of the United Church, shared some wisdom with me. "Ralph," he said, "choose one or two causes that you can really give yourself to. Work as hard as you can for those. As for the other causes and issues, know enough so you don't get in the way."

A few samples

Here are a few samples of things people have in mind when they ask, "What does the United Church have to say about the ills and struggles of our world?" Quite a lot, as it turns out. You could fill a library on any one of these issues, so don't consider what follows any more than a quick run-through. If you'd like

to chase down the details of anything that follows in this chapter, check out the United Church Commons on the national church website: www.united-church.ca. It's a library full of statements and study documents.

Addictions

Smoking is harmful to health, both for those who smoke and for others around them. Many folks are allergic to tobacco smoke, and smokers usually have an "aura" about them. Other than saying that it's a Christian responsibility to take care of the body, and to be concerned about the welfare of others, the United Church hasn't said much about smoking.

There was a time when many people (myself included) smoked. Not anymore. In my home congregation, there's no smoking anywhere in the building. As is the case in any public building.

Booze is certainly the big one. It's far more of a social problem than drugs, hard or soft. It causes untold misery and costs us millions. I have no statistics about this, but I know there are a lot of recovering alcoholics among our members. And some alcoholics who have *not* recovered. Many congregations have Alcoholics Anonymous, Al-Anon or Ala-teen groups that use their facilities regularly.

The official United Church position is that abstinence from alcohol is the "wisest and safest course," but moderate usage is okay. Probably the majority of United Church people enjoy a glass of wine before dinner or a beer on a hot summer day.

We probably panicked a bit when marijuana first hit us in the 1960s. Some experts say it's less harmful than alcohol or tobacco. As I write this, the legality of recreational marijuana is before Parliament, and the prime minister has said it will be legalized.

How will we, as a church, feel about that? We know that it creates many of the same problems as alcohol. So I wouldn't be surprised if United Church people have a similar attitude toward marijuana as they do toward alcohol.

Hard drugs are a major social hazard that cause all kinds of personal consequences for the user, and a variety of social problems. The "drug problem" is a very complex issue that's getting worse every year. Education and law enforcement don't seem to be working. The United Church has been saying to governments, "look at the underlying causes and work on those. Don't just treat the symptoms."

Prescription drugs are legal and respectable, and may well be doing more damage to more people than all the others. They provide a quick, easy, but very temporary way out of life's difficulties. And there are social addictions such as workaholism, gambling and shopping which are part of the same picture. Workaholism is the one I have the most trouble with.

Real answers come to us as we straighten out the problems in our lives that make us turn to these things. It takes more courage to face up to life and ourselves than to pop a pill or pour a shot of scotch.

Hard answers, which point to long-term changes, force us to turn to our faith. Not for an instant "miracle," but for the courage our faith provides, and for the support and counsel the church community can give.

Gambling

We were caught napping on this one. When casinos and lotteries were legalized in the 1960s and 1970s, only a few of our people yelled.

The church has always said that gambling is wrong. But many United Church people don't see a problem with spend-

ing a few dollars on a lottery ticket or on a Saturday night bingo, especially when the proceeds go to a good cause. Others feel quite strongly that gambling is a significant social problem.

As casinos and bingo parlours are opening all over, more and more people in the United Church are pointing out that the folks who do the most gambling are the ones who can least afford it. For many, gambling is an addiction that's harder to handle than booze or dope.

The United Church has said that it's not a good idea to accept money raised from gambling, tempting as that may be. Some people think that's silly. Others agree that it's wrong to raise money, even for worthy causes, by using other people's weaknesses and addictions. They point out that in order for someone to win a lottery, a whole lot of people have to lose. Often more than money.

As you can tell, I don't like gambling in general and lotteries in particular. That's a minority opinion, I grant you. Congregations are usually bound by their own collective conscience, and some have used lottery money.

Sex

It would be so easy for the church to use the "Who cares?" method of decision-making on this one. Or even the "Right's right!" way. There are plenty of people who want the church to say only one word on the subject: "No!"

That kind of response never worked and it isn't appropriate today. It's foolish to ignore the fact that teenagers become sexually active very early; that living together has become common, even respectable; and that the "no sex before marriage" ideal is no longer honoured in Canadian society. Most couples coming to be married in the church are already living together.

You'll find many responses to all this in the church. I still

believe that lifelong commitment *in marriage*, and the fidelity that goes with it, is the way God calls us to be. Others say that it's the commitment, the caring, the life-giving relationship that's important, not the legality of marriage. Whether that's between couples of the same or opposite sex.

I believe United Church people would say that sex is not "bad." It isn't dirty. It is beautiful and fulfilling. My personal sense is that when sex is an expression of love and commitment, it is a sacrament.

But yes, sex can also be dangerous, destructive, and exploitative.

The rainbow community

The United Church struggled mightily over gender identities and sexual orientations for many years, but I think the matter is finally settled. That's not to say that we have universal agreement. Some are still fighting angrily against it.

It is now clear from official statements and, more importantly, from the attitude expressed by the majority of United Church people, that sexual orientation and gender identity really have no bearing on full participation in our community. That includes the order of ministry. We're gradually learning that homosexual people can also live in caring, loving, committed relationships.

Some of our most effective ministers are gay, lesbian, or transgendered – as are our current and previous moderators, the highest elected position you can achieve in our church.

This is not to say that gay, lesbian, and transgendered people don't get hassled in church, sometimes. Fortunately, however, it is happening less and less, and more and more they are being accepted as individuals who, like all the rest of us, are created in the image of God.

Abortion

Here the United Church has made a statement, though it hasn't always been accurately reported.

We are *not* "in favour of abortion." I don't know anyone in the United Church who has ever made that kind of statement, even though the Church has been quoted as having said that.

What we have said is that *there are some situations in which abortion is the lesser of two evils.* When all the available solutions to a problem are bad, you pick the one that is least bad.

The United Church position is, basically, that there are times when abortion is necessary and that it is up to the woman and her doctor to decide when that is.

Abortion is not a substitute for birth control. On that everyone agrees, I think. But a vocal minority in the church says "no" to abortion under any circumstances. To them, abortion is killing, plain and simple.

Divorce

The United Church is not in favour of divorce either. But, again, it is the least bad thing in many instances.

It's true that many couples simply pack it in when the going gets a bit rough, instead of working at their commitment, getting help with their problems, and struggling to build a better relationship. Many people are far too casual about marriage commitments.

But to say "No divorce, ever!" would be condemning some people to a living hell. To rule that if you've been divorced you can never marry again is equally harsh.

That's why so many refugees from other denominations come to the United Church to be married and why we have so many "blended families." Our clergy often spend long hours helping people who come from other denominations with a

great burden of guilt and hurt. Some ministers feel quite angry when they see the shattered faith of people who have had rule books thrown at them.

Abuse

In the last several decades, we became acutely aware of the extent to which sexual, psychological, and physical abuse happens in families, often in families that seem to present a picture of respectability. It also happens in various clubs, athletic organizations, and other helping groups. And it happens in churches of every denomination, more than most of us want to admit. Women, children, and the elderly are the most frequent victims.

Many churches, along with other groups such as the Scouts, sports organizations and others, now insist that volunteers who work with others who may be at risk (mostly children and seniors), must have a police record check before they begin this work. That includes the clergy and other church professionals.

I find it very sad that this is necessary. But it is. There's certainly no watertight solution, but there is help from conference and from the national church offices to show congregations and their leaders how to protect the more vulnerable ones in their care.

The traditional response of the United Church (and pretty well every other church and organization) had been to sweep such problems under the carpet. Now we have come to recognize that we have a moral and legal responsibility to name abuse and work to prevent it. It's important to deal firmly with the aggressors, and gently and pastorally with the victims. To look the other way is to be a party to the crime.

The United Church was one of the first denominations to work on ways to deal with sexual harassment and abuse, and

one of the first denominations to publish resources to help ministers and congregations to name sexual violence and minister to victims, survivors, and perpetrators. We've put into place some tough policies and procedures so that we can act on abuse quickly and appropriately. It's not perfect, of course, but I am proud of the way my church has faced this head on. It hurt, but it was absolutely necessary.

It's my personal opinion that male adults (like me) have a particular responsibility to work on this problem, because most often it's male adults who have been the abusers. The good news is that the level of safety and awareness that has been created for vulnerable people is unprecedented.

Forgiveness

It's not just the vulnerable ones that need protecting of course. Leaders need to be protected against false accusations, and there needs to be a way of offering forgiveness and second chances to those who have made mistakes in the past.

I have a friend who spent time in jail because he had embezzled money from his company. When he came out of jail, he was invited by another friend to come to church. My friend knew he needed help to get his life together. He made no secret of the fact that he had been in jail for embezzling money. He became active in the congregation, and they, in a great act of Christian trust, asked him to be the church treasurer. He didn't let them down.

Some years ago in our church, an elderly man was paroled after serving time for sexual abuse of children. We could have excluded him from the church, of course, but we welcomed him back instead. God forgives, and God's people must forgive. He became part of the church community, but we set up a firm but informal system where we made sure he was never

by himself at any time anywhere in the church. There were no problems.

Crime and punishment

The United Church has an official position against taking human life as a means of punishment. Its reasons are simple. Humans don't have the right to make that kind of irrevocable judgment.

Killing is wrong, for whatever reason. Furthermore, it doesn't prevent crime. There is no evidence anywhere that capital punishment prevents others from killing.

That official position is quite clear even though some United Church people feel that, in the case of the killing of law officers, the penalty should be death.

Our official church stand on capital punishment springs out of our general attitude toward the way we handle those people who violate our laws. After looking at the way Jesus related to people who were in trouble with the law, the church has said that the purpose of our justice system should be to turn people around to a better way of life. It should never be used to get even. Revenge should not be confused with "finding closure."

The church also points to a fact that is easily documented by studying trial records. Those who have money and connections are treated much better by the law than those who don't.

Censorship

All of us realize that television, particularly, and mass media in general, affect the way we think and act far more than we dare to admit. Those who claim it doesn't affect them at all should think about the billions of dollars companies spend on advertising. They hire some of the sharpest minds and most effective

organizations to study which advertising works, and for whom. If advertising didn't translate into sales, companies wouldn't spend a nickel on it. The question really is, do we want to be affected that way?

The Saskatchewan Conference of the United Church came out strongly against "the present proliferation of advertising." They claimed "the values propagated by some advertising and the gospel preached by the church, are in direct conflict."

It's not just the advertisements that influence us. The programs do, too. Many of us are worried about the increasing violence and exploitative sex that occupies so much TV time. For others, the concerns go deeper and include role-stereotyping, superficial news reporting, manipulation of children, and, most of all, advertisers who use our fears to sell us products.

Nor have we really come to terms with the social, spiritual, and ethical problems of social media. Geezers like me have really no idea what this is all about, except that we're aware of abuse, manipulation, bullying, misinformation, and a host of other issues. My job, as a senior who doesn't use or understand social media, is to encourage my grandchildren and others to look carefully, think analytically, and act responsibly.

What we've not figured out is how to do something about media abuse, without violating our fundamental freedom of expression. As a culture, the pendulum has swung hard in the direction of personal freedom, and it needs to move back a bit toward the concept of personal and social responsibility.

Caring for creation

"Everybody is in favour of ecology," a young enthusiast once told me, as if that was like being in favour of motherhood.

Actually, ecology is a very fundamental issue for Christians. It's about our relationship to the world God created and gave

to us to care for. Ecology is as much an attitude as a science. It's a way of seeing ourselves as deeply connected to everything on this whole planet.

Sometimes we think of the world as God's body, and polluting the air as the fouling of God's breath, God's Spirit. It means that ecological concerns are part of the same fabric as personal morality, social concerns, and international justice issues.

All of us share a common, human tendency. We love to get riled up about mistakes other people are making. It's way more fun getting into a sweat over Brazilian rain forests than about the way we use lumber and paper. After all, if we stop cutting trees here in Canada, that'll cost us jobs. Saving the rain forest costs jobs in Brazil, too, the jobs of people who have no unemployment insurance or welfare.

Limits to growth

One of these days the penny will drop. Ecology costs. Jobs, money, standard of living. It's good not to use Styrofoam cups in church and to recycle our newspapers. But those are two-bit responses to multi-billion dollar problems.

We are not going to do anything significant about the ecology of our planet until we take a radical drop in our standard of living. Us, here in Canada. You and me. Not the people in the Third World. Their standard of living is already ecologically responsible. They have no choice.

If we want healthy food to eat, clean air to breathe and water to drink, it's going to cost us.

Christians have a good word to use here: stewardship. A steward is someone who takes gentle care of something that belongs to someone else. We are stewards of God's creation. Even more, we are invited to participate in that creation be-

cause God loves us and trusts us to deal kindly with it.

Because of our growing concern, and because we were asked to do this by our First Nations members, a new line "to live with respect in Creation" was added to our creed.

Politics

There has never been a time when the church wasn't involved in politics. The Bible is often more political than religious, although in biblical days people didn't really distinguish between the two. Jesus was very political.

It wasn't until the Reformation, when people were reacting against the strong political power of the Roman Catholic Church, that the idea of separating church and state came along.

The United Church has never had political power, but it has always had political influence. It has never been able to deliver a block of votes to any candidate. Nor has it ever tried or even wanted to.

For many years, there has been a disagreement between the evangelical and the liberal elements in our church. The liberal group feels that the church not only has a right, it has an *obligation* to speak out. We have to change the systems that put people down, and to do that involves politics. The evangelical group feels you must begin by changing people. People then go out and change oppressive systems. There is truth in both positions.

Often, the church speaks out through petitions and resolutions from presbyteries, conferences, and other church bodies. I don't really think that does any good, although it does make us feel as if we've done something.

We do that a lot less now than we used to. We've realized that the church simply doesn't have the political influence it had, even a few years ago. We've got to find other ways to speak to the social and political process, and to more actively encour-

age people to think and act responsibly and courageously as citizens.

Militarism

Everybody is against war. The big question is how do you prevent it?

People sitting in United Church pews represent a variety of viewpoints. Many of them share the view of the military establishment and say the only way to prevent war is to be so strong nobody will attack you. Therefore, you must have superior weapons. The military is a necessary evil.

Many others in the United Church will say this results in an insane escalation of armaments all over the world, which could easily end in the total destruction of our planet. Nobody would win. Everybody would lose.

Besides, if the money and energy put into building bigger and better weapons were put into solving problems, like poverty for instance, we could head off potential wars. If we took the money now going into armaments and spent it on a better lifestyle for the Third World, and to address the huge ecological concerns facing our planet, we could do that work (which would generate lots of jobs) and have money left over. Everybody would win!

Terrorism has traumatized nations, governments, and individual people. It's well and good to ask our police and military to discover and prevent terrorist attacks, but that does not address the underlying problem. I have no particular qualifications to offer solutions, but I am sure the solution will not come from putting more guns in people's hands.

It's also important to remember that terrorism is not something that radical Muslims invented. Radical Christians and Jews and various others have been using terrorism for centuries.

Aboriginal relations

Through the years, the church has had a history of supporting people who had somebody else's foot on their necks. Some of these groups are overseas. Some are right here in Canada.

One minority asking for their rights are Canada's first peoples, the First Nations. Many within the church have felt a strong call to support our aboriginal sisters and brothers in their struggle for what they see as basic human rights. The United Church has taken strong official stands and unofficial action in this regard.

For many years, the United Church and several other denominations worked with the federal government to operate a number of residential schools, where First Nations' children were sent. The stated intent was to give these young people the skills they would need so they could take their place in our economy. But the underlying motive was to make them over in our own Anglo-Saxon image. At that time, the dominant white power structure thought that was a good idea. "The white man's burden," was a phrase often used. The tragic result was that we stripped them of their culture, their identity, their language, and their pride.

The United Church has issued formal apologies to First Nations people, in 1986 and 1998, because we became aware that even with our best intentions, we were part of what some have called "cultural genocide."

Most of the teachers and administrators in the residential schools were good and kind people, and genuinely wanted the best for their students. I don't think we have a right to be critical of them.

They walked by the light they had. They were part of a society that was convinced that the best way to help First Nations people and other cultural minorities was to educate them into the dominant society.

It was this conviction that drove much of the world mission movement until a few decades ago. We now recognize the destructiveness of that attitude, but the blame (if there must be blame) rests on our whole society.

But that's not the most painful part of the story. There were a few teachers and administrators who physically and sexually abused the children in their charge. This was wrong then as it is wrong now.

It is a traumatic time for the United Church. We genuinely want justice to be done. The Truth and Reconciliation Commission showed us some of the big steps that need to be taken toward that justice.

To find out more about that commission, Google "Truth and Reconciliation Commission," or check the the national United Church website. Kairos Canada also has an excellent resource called "Strength for Climbing" on its website.

World outreach

We've always been a strong missionary church. Sometimes we've tried to "convert" people in other parts of the world to our way of thinking. More often, we've tried to work beside them in their struggles to grow and develop.

The question is much larger than simply giving money. The United Church believes we should act politically and economically here in Canada to support our neighbours in other parts of the world. It isn't just a matter of giving aid. It's a matter of changing some of the systems of trade, economic control, and industrial power that keep us rich and them poor.

As long as the world's economy is structured in such a way that we maintain our privileges at the expense of others, we can't expect them to be grateful for the bit of aid we offer – or to expect our aid to do much good.

Sexism

Another group that has been denied fair treatment, even though they're not a minority, is women. Most United Church people would agree with the principle that men and women should be treated equally. There should be equal opportunity and equal pay for equal work. However, we don't all agree on what needs rearranging in order to make this happen.

Within the United Church, a vocal minority of men and women say the issue is very close to the heart of our faith. Sexism restricts us to playing a "role." We are pushed into thinking and behaving in ways that society prescribes, rather than developing individually as free children of God.

Concerns around sexism amount to far more than simply changing "chairman" to "chairperson," though that's important, too. It's a question of who we truly are as people made in the "image of God" our Creator, who is neither male nor female.

Depending on your point of view, the United Church is either "capitulating to strident feminists" or "making progress toward human liberation" more quickly than most other groups.

As a society and as a church, we've made huge progress toward equality of the sexes, but perhaps because of that we've been forgetting about the issues involved, and possibly losing some of the ground we've gained.

Among other things, we're getting a bit careless in our use of exclusive language. And because significant advances have been made, we're assuming the battle has been won. Women are still not treated equally in a whole lot of ways, wage levels being just one of them.

Churchgoer values

A study done by Reginald Bibby of the University of Lethbridge showed that the values of church people generally (and United Church people in particular) didn't differ much from the rest of the Canadian population. I found that a very sad commentary on the Christian church.

Bibby has a point. A very large segment of the church population come Sunday by Sunday for a kind of "verbal massage." It feels good to be in church. It's comforting to hear the old hymns and listen to the Bible being read. And, if you don't listen too closely, even the sermon is comforting. So nothing you hear or do in church really affects how you live your life.

On either side of this majority we have an enthusiastic minority – some on the "evangelical right" and others on the "social action left." If Bibby had measured those two groups, the most committed 20 percent rather than the majority at the centre, he would, I'm convinced, have found some differences.

That's not just hopeful conjecture. Unless Canadians are very different from Americans in this regard, significant church involvement *does* make a difference. The Gallup research organization found that people deeply involved in churches and synagogues are three times more active than others in social, charitable, and civic activities such as feeding the hungry, housing the homeless, and caring for the sick.

A Pew Research Center study of the ways religion influences the daily lives of Americans finds that people who are highly religious are more engaged with their extended families, more likely to volunteer, more involved in their communities, and generally happier with the way things are going in their lives.

To soar like an eagle

It seems that it's the intensity of the involvement, not whether you're "conservative" or "liberal," that counts. And that's consistent with what Jesus taught. He didn't care a whole lot about the kind of theology we espoused. He was more concerned about what kind of life we lived. "You'll know them by the fruit they produce," he said.

There's a lot of vitality in the church, and we see it often in those who are most liberal and those who are most conservative. These two groups in our church have the stuff that could get a lot of jaded pew-sitters off dead centre. But they'll never do that until they learn to listen to each other and recognize that each has a valuable element of the gospel that the other has missed.

I think we may have forgotten how to see the value in our differences. But I see some signs that we're beginning to relearn it. I hope I'm right. If I'm wrong, then the United Church of Canada may have lost its sense of inclusiveness and, perhaps, its reason for being.

Alone, the right and left wings of the United Church flop around on the ground, unable to fly. And the rest of the world doesn't hear our statements and resolutions and sermons. They just see us flailing away at each other. "What a bunch of turkeys!" they think.

If we could love and respect each other through our differences – if we were prepared to listen and learn from each other – we could, as the prophet Isaiah said, "renew our strength," and "mount up with wings like eagles."

We could do miracles!

12

The Impossible Dream

For where two or three are gathered in my name,
I am there among them.
Matthew 18:20

It feels as if it was just a few years ago. I was at a service of worship in Vernon, an hour's drive from my home. It was a meeting of the BC Conference of the United Church. At the end of that service, I was to be inducted as the president of the conference. A little bit like a bishop.

We were receiving communion. With me in the worship were my son-in-law, Don, and my first grandchild, Jake, who was just a year old. "May I give Jake his first communion?" I asked Don. "Sure, Grandpa!" he said, smiling broadly.

As I held Jake in my arms, I broke off a piece of the bread, dipped it in the wine, and put it in Jake's mouth. At that moment, I was overwhelmed by a prayer I found deep inside myself.

"God, when Jake grows to be a young man, let there be a strong and vigorous and faith-filled church that he can be part of. If he chooses too.

"But, God, if that isn't possible, let the church move into the future with vigour and enthusiasm and power, so that if it goes down in flames, I can say to Jake, 'You should have been there. That was my church, Jake, and it bet everything on the future. It went down in flames, but it was a glorious struggle.'

"But, God, please don't make me have to tell Jake that the church just slowly faded away, and the last we heard of it was a weak little whimper. Please, God. I don't want to tell that story to Jake."

Well, Jake is a young man now. And there has been a dynamic, faith-filled congregation that has nurtured him and the other members of his family.

Twenty years ago, I thought my church was barely breathing and on life-support. I'm pleased to tell you that I was wrong. This United Church of mine is still struggling on. It didn't go down in flames or die with a whimper. It's older. A bit smaller. Important things have changed. But there's still life pulsing vigorously through its veins.

So my prayer has changed. Now I pray that Jake, years from now when he is an old man, will thank God for a church that has nurtured and loved him and helped him grow, as it did for me.

Depth, diversity, and despair

I'm more optimistic about the United Church now than I was 20 years ago. Numbers keep falling as they have for virtually

every denomination right across the theological spectrum. The huge mega-churches that attracted so much envy a couple of decades ago are now in trouble. The famed Crystal Cathedral declared bankruptcy, then was sold.

It may be that people are looking at the church a bit differently. We may have fewer members, but more adherents – people who participate actively in the life of the church without formally joining. I think that's probably true in the congregation where I worship.

It's not that I think the church is out of trouble. But I think, for the most part, we've stopped wringing our hands and asking, "What are we doing wrong?"

Updating this book for the fourth time has been a most interesting exercise. To make sure it connects with United Church people across the country, I sent the manuscript to almost three dozen reviewers who commented on the draft and offered suggestions.

Out of that came two very strong impressions. They arose from the tone of the replies, more than the information they supplied.

The first one is that the United Church is even more diverse now that it was when I wrote those first three editions of *This United Church of Ours*. What's more, that diversity is good. It's a delight. It's a strength.

Second, I felt a growing sense of comfort. "We are what we are!" seemed to be the attitude that came across to me in those replies. We have a noble heritage of courage and foresight, of reaching out to those who are hurting. And I sense a kind of inner integrity. We're not beating up on ourselves the way we've done in the past.

Those reviewers were not papering over the problems that hit us in the face – problems of finance, of organization, of relevance, of leadership, of crumbling buildings. Those prob-

lems are real and could bring us down.

But let's put all that in context. I've done a lot of gigs on what used to be called "the rubber chicken circuit" – service clubs, interest groups, many kinds of organizations. Currently I am a member of the local photo club.

All of them have essentially the same problems as the churches. Social scientists tell us that, in North America at least, there was a fundamental shift that happened during the turbulent 1960s. It was a shift away from trust in authority figures, a loss of confidence in government, business, and private organizations of every kind. This may be why many people participate in the life of the church without committing to a formal membership.

In other words, what's been happening in the churches has its roots in society as a whole, and doesn't necessarily have much to do with the way we function as a church.

Erosion of authority and community

A number of social scientists have written on this. One of them pinpoints the watershed – the symbolic moment. It was when a young protester put a flower in the muzzle of a soldier's gun during a demonstration at the Pentagon in 1967. I vividly remember seeing that photograph, which symbolized a significant change in our social attitudes.

Most social scientists agree that from the 1960s onward, there has been a steady erosion of commitment to organizations and respect for authority. Less and less do we see ourselves as part of a group or country or church. More and more we see ourselves as individuals. And we have far less faith and trust in our leaders. Leaders of any kind – political, medical, athletic, religious, and community. But that individualism can lead to loneliness, and loneliness into depression.

Author Charles Montgomery is quoted in *The United Church Observer* as saying, "Social isolation just may be the greatest environmental hazard of city living." And most of us live in cities.

"Loneliness is as harmful to health as smoking 15 cigarettes a day," the magazine goes on to say. "It hikes the risk of dementia by 64 percent. Loneliness is a quantifiable health hazard."

There are all kinds of indicators that the majority of people in Canada consider themselves Christians. An even higher percentage will say "Yes" when the pollster asks them if they believe in God. Genuine atheists are really hard to find. There's also a deep interest in things religious. The media often give prime coverage to a story about religion, especially if there is an element of controversy around it.

What most of us don't realize is that a life of faith, lived in a community of faith, is probably the best antidote to the disease of loneliness that exists. Chaeyoon Lim, of the University of Wisconsin, quoted in *The United Church Observer*, says that "people who are religiously involved report a higher level of life satisfaction, as well as better mental and physical health." In other words, you and I need the church. Our society needs the church.

Scientific leapfrogs

I don't do predictions. I'm not going to try to tell you what the church will be like in the next few decades. But I am convinced that the human animal is incurably religious. In the years since the development of the scientific method, and the huge leaps of technological innovation, some pundits have been predicting the total demise of religion. But it hasn't happened. Far from it.

In fact, as scientific developments have leapfrogged over

each other, and as science has become in itself a kind of religion, humans are hungering for deeper answers than science can provide.

Science can see facts. The human spirit can see truth. They don't contradict each other. Both are necessary and life giving.

Truth and fact

Bev and I were on a rickety old school bus travelling on a logging road up a mountain in Alaska. We got off to admire a field of wildflowers. Our leader, a botanist, described the various blossoms and how they fit into the ecology of the area.

All of a sudden, she squealed in delight and dropped to her knees. She pointed to a tiny blue flower. "Look at that!" she cried. "Isn't it beautiful? Isn't it glorious? I haven't seen one of those in years. This is so wonderful." That was her human spirit delighting in the glory of a tiny, blue flower.

After a while, she stood up, still smiling, and gave us some information about that flower and how it fit into the scheme of things and why its discovery was important. That was the botanist speaking.

She wasn't contradicting herself. She spoke truth when she cried, "Isn't it beautiful?" She spoke fact when she described its place in the ecology of that field.

I am what science fiction writers call a "cyborg." That's a combination of technology and human flesh that develops extraordinary powers. Those of us who are older remember a TV series called *The Six-Million Dollar Man*, about a somewhat improbable cyborg.

I don't claim any extraordinary powers, but I have had the lenses in both eyes replaced. And I wear a pacemaker, which keeps my heart beating. I also swallow a handful of pills every morning.

That technology, and a lively, caring congregation of faithful people at First United Church in Kelowna, have me feeling hale and hearty and able to tackle a book like this, even though I'm well into the "old fogey" category.

A mystery

If there's any wisdom that comes with age, it goes something like this. It is not just science that is keeping me alive. It's something like a synergy that happens when the power of science, the power of faith, and the support of a community work together in the human life.

I am wise enough to know that, as a human being, I am more than the sum of my parts, that I am a miracle of creation assisted by the technology of science. That's a wisdom to which all of creation is called – to celebrate together the joy of creation and the dazzle of science. Only then can these miracles work together to green the world, rather than turn it into ashes.

Such wisdom is not learned in schools. It is God given, and very near the heart of what we call religion or spirituality. It is at the heart of mystery.

"Mystery" is a very powerful, very spiritual idea. As I wrote earlier, it is not a puzzle to be solved. It is a reality that we reflect on, dream about, discuss, experience, and proclaim. In the depth of that mystery is the hunger, the yearning, we humans have for something more than food, water, and shelter. We long for deeper relationships with others. We long for people to love, and we long to be loved by others.

Longing for the holy

We long for a reality beyond the frantic and conflicted life most of us live day to day. We search for the holy, the numinous, the spiritual. Why we do that is part of the mystery, although I know

a very old story that tells how humans are made in the image and likeness of God.

The story comes right at the beginning of a very old and precious book that tells of other people, in other troubled times, who have searched for and sometimes experienced God. You can read that story yourself – in the Bible.

In that quest for the holy, every human society has generated a religion of some sort. That yearning for God has not gone away, even though, here in Canada at least, many no longer go searching for God in churches. But they still go searching.

Humans can't help it. There is something built into our basic fibre that has us searching for meaning, for the holy. Because of that deep, visceral yearning, we will grow a church of some kind because we can't live without it. It may have a very different name and a vastly different way of worshipping and working. But there will be a community of searchers who will gather sometimes to tell each other where they have found spiritual food for their journey – where they have encountered the holy in their lives – and to cry and laugh together through the joy and pain of life.

A new church will be generated out of the past, generated out of our life experiences as we struggle to stay human in a technological, consumer society.

There is a church for me, right now, in this last decade of my life. It is the church I have struggled to describe in this book. And I pray that my grandchildren will find some such community of faith in the technocratic world they will live in, for what might be 100 or more years of life.

Whether that faith community will resemble the United Church of Canada – whether it will be a continuation of today's church or something totally new – I don't know. But there will be a church, if we approach the future with courage and generosity and an openness to the mystery.

The changing church

I was astounded when Wood Lake Publishing editor Mike Schwartzentruber asked me to do a fourth edition of *This United Church of Ours*. It seemed like such a short time since I'd done the third edition, and I remembered how many changes there had been in our denomination since it was published in 2000.

I remember the ancient curse, "May you live in interesting times." I have no doubt that the next several dozen years will be "interesting" for all of us, and certainly interesting for the church.

Since you have read this far in this book, I am assuming that you have some interest in a church that will be 100 years old in 2025. What kind of a church will it be?

We can only guess. We can mine the past for ideas and inspiration, but we will create the new church out of the future, and we never know what that future is until it is upon us.

Is it worth it?

What it all boils down to in the end is, why bother? Certainly, we could use a sleep-in on Sunday morning. We have enough to do without running off to church events all week. Expenses are plenty high without somebody holding an offering plate under our noses. There are plenty of questions to bug us without adding "What does God want?" to the list.

Most of us don't gain much social status from being part of a church. We don't get brownie points for being Christian. There may be a few business contacts, but it's hardly worth it. Church-going Christians are very much a minority group. And, according to the values of the marketplace, we're losers.

I began going to church in the first place while I was a "jock" at a local radio station, doing an open-line show. *Ralph's Party Line*, they called it. One of the first open-line shows in Canada.

We advertised used cars, soap, deodorant, and breakfast cereal – everything I needed to clean me up, make me smell nice, fill my belly, and take me somewhere. But I didn't have anything important to go to. Like every young male struggling to get ahead in the world, I was "all stressed up with no place to go."

I didn't have any great, flashing-lights conversion. I'm not saying those "born-again" experiences don't happen to people or that they are not valid. I'm just saying that nothing like that happened to me. As I've been nurtured in the church, I find myself really appreciating the gift of faith given me by the people in it.

So I genuinely believe that in our tired and sometimes hurting tradition – building on the heritage of faith we've received – we can find some (not all) of the building blocks for a new church that will evolve, or perhaps arise like the phoenix from the ashes of the old.

Why doesn't somebody do something?

It's a lonely world out there in "the jungle." So many people seem to be on the make and it can be difficult to find and make genuine friendships. But I find, when I'm with my friends in church, I'm not trying to prove as much.

I see the young families in church, struggling to build a future for their children, and I remember when my kids were small and how Bev and I struggled. I worry about the children. All of them. Every parent does.

I remember how I wanted my kids to be part of something where there were other adults and other kids willing to talk about significant things. I knew that just dropping my kids off at Sunday school would give them a double message about how important I thought my faith really was, so for the sake of my

kids (among many other reasons), I became involved in the church.

Did it pay off for me? That's probably the wrong question, because parenting (or life in general for that matter) is not something you do for the "payoff." But I'm delighted when I see in my kids (they're middle-aged now!) a strong sense of values of what is right and wrong.

Living in relationship

Bev and I have a pretty stable relationship right now, but it hasn't always been that way, and we'll probably hit some rocky times again. One of the things that's really helped is being part of a number of study groups in the church.

None of them were about marriage, but it's surprising how much of what we talked about related to home and family life. Aside from some good ideas, it was good to know that other people had the same kinds of problems. That kind of support is invaluable.

These groups were also an excellent place to get to know people in other situations: people who were divorced or widowed, single parents, those who remarried, those who never married. I learned from the lives they've lived. Bev and I learned how to make a marriage work during the routine hassles, when everybody is going in a different direction. Or at three in the morning, when somebody's barfing their guts out.

Most important of all, we found friends we could call when our lives seemed to be falling apart. Friends who came and listened to our anger and our fear.

It is through the church that I first found friends who were comfortable telling me they were gay, lesbian, or transgendered. They had patience with me while I worked through my deep, inherited, ingrained homophobia – until I could see them as

strong, creative, individuals with a deep sense of morality and faith.

To dream the impossible dream

There's another reason I'm in the church – a reason that's bigger than all of the other reasons, though it's connected somehow. When my writing is going well and Bev and I are getting along fine, there's still a hole in there – kind of a hunger. And when things are not going well, that hunger becomes a sharp pain.

Sometimes, when I'm out on a walk or lying in bed waiting for sleep, I dream an impossible dream. I have a dream, a sense of God calling again and again, asking me to do something with my life. In that dream, my life is deeply important to God.

At first, my ego tells me that means God is calling me to do something that'll attract worldwide attention. To be a hero. To be famous. That turns out to be *my* dream, not God's.

If I stay with God's impossible dream, I feel a simple call to live creatively and caringly. To be the most creative and thoughtful person I can be within the limits of my age and declining health. To take time to talk with the neighbours and actually *listen* to what they say. To think less selfishly when I decide how to vote. To live in a more caring relationship with God's creation.

When I respond to that dream, I discover that it's my own need that motivates me. When I respond with creativity and caring to the loneliness of my neighbours, for example, in church and otherwise, I answer my *own* desperate need.

When I have that dream, I can believe the improbable teaching that God loves me – that I am important to God. Specifically me. Ralph. With a splitting headache, sweaty palms, and a zit on the end of my nose. When the dream fades, I know I

need more time in prayer and meditation or, sometimes, long conversations with friends in the church. Sometimes a walk in the green glory of nature.

The dream means life

So much of the time, it seems impossible that God considers me, and those insignificant relationships, to be part of a holy and creative purpose. It is so much easier to see all of life as petty and pointless, a pitiful bunch of humans thrashing around till we destroy ourselves and the planet with us.

And yet sometimes when I share that dream with friends, they tell me they also dream God's impossible dream. They tell me what I already know – that the dream is shared by people of faith, many kinds of faith, all over the world.

If the dream is delusion, then it is a wonderful, creative, hopeful delusion. Far more satisfying than any "reality." If the dream is truth, then it is the only truth worth struggling for.

They tell me what I already know, that the dream is nurtured, given life and purpose and focus, in the community of faith we call the church. They tell me that to dream God's impossible dream means life!

I know of no better place to dream the impossible dream, than in this United Church of ours.

CONTACT INFORMATION

GENERAL COUNCIL OFFICES
3250 Bloor St., Suite 300, Etobicoke, ON M8X 2Y4
Telephone: 416-231-5931 Toll free: 1-800-268-3871
Email: info@united-church.ca
Website: http://united-church.ca

ALBERTA AND NORTHWEST CONFERENCE
9911 48 Ave. NW, Edmonton, AB T6E 5V6
Telephone: 780-435-3995 / 780-438-3317
Email: kjackson@anwconf.com
Website: http://albertanorthwestconference.ca

ALL NATIVE CIRCLE CONFERENCE
367 Selkirk Ave., Winnipeg, MB R2W 2M3
Telephone: 204-582-5518 / 204-582-6649
Email: admin@ancc.united-churca.ca
Website: http://allnativecircleconference.ca

BAY OF QUINTE CONFERENCE
25 Holloway St., Belleville, ON K8P 1N8
Telephone: 613-967-0150 / 613-967-1934 / 1-888-759-2444
Email: officeadmin@bayofquinteconference.ca
Website: http://bayofquinteconference.ca

BRITISH COLUMBIA CONFERENCE
4383 Rumble St., Burnaby, BC V5J 2A2
Telephone: 604-431-0434 / 604-431-0439 / 1-800-934-0434
Email: reception@bc.united-church.ca
Website: http://bc.united-church.ca

HAMILTON CONFERENCE
P. O. Box 100, Carlisle, ON L0R 1H0
Telephone: 905-659-3343 / 905-659-7766
Email: office@hamconf.org
Website: http://hamconf.org

LONDON CONFERENCE
P. O. Box 28039, London, ON N6H 5E1
Telephone: 519-672-1930 / 519-439-2800
Email: office@londonconference.ca
Website: http://londonconference.ca

MANITOBA AND NORTHWESTERN ONTARIO CONFERENCE
1622-B St. Mary's Rd., Winnipeg, MB R2M 3W7
Telephone: 204-233-8911 / 204-233-3289
Email: office@confmnwo.mb.ca
Website: http://mnwo.ca

MANITOU CONFERENCE
319 McKenzie Ave., North Bay, ON P1B 7E3
Telephone: 705-474-3350 / 705-497-3597
Email: office@manitouconference.ca
Website: http://manitouconference.ca

MARITIME CONFERENCE
21 Wright St., Sackville, NB E4L 4P8
Telephone: 506-536-1334 / 506-536-2900
Email: info@marconf.ca
Website: http://marconf.ca

MONTREAL AND OTTAWA CONFERENCE
225 50E Ave, Lachine, QC H8T 2T7
Telephone: 514-634-7015 ext. 21 / 514-634-2489
Email: moconferenceuccmtl@gmail.com
Website: http://montrealandottawaconference.ca

NEWFOUNDLAND AND LABRADOR CONFERENCE
320 Elizabeth Ave., St. John's, NL A1B 1T9
Telephone: 709-754-0386 / 709-754-8336
Email: unitedchurch@nfld.net
Website: http://newlabconf.com

SASKATCHEWAN CONFERENCE
418A McDonald St., Regina, SK S4N 6E1
Telephone: 306-721-3311 / 306-721-3171
Email: ucskco@skconf.ca
Website: http://sk.united-church.ca

TORONTO CONFERENCE
65 Mayall Ave., Downsview, ON M3L 1E7
Telephone: 416-241-9698 / 416-241-2689
Email: tco-office@united-church.ca
Website: http://torontoconference.ca

SUGGESTED READING

Airhart, Phyllis D. *A Church with the Soul of a Nation: Making and Remaking the United Church of Canada.* McGill-Queen's University Press, 2014.

Borg, Marcus. *Reading the Bible Again for the First Time: Taking the Bible Seriously but not Literally.* San Francisco: Harper San Francisco, 2001.

Graham, Rochelle, Flora Litt, and Wayne Irwin. *Healing from the Heart: A Guide to Christian Healing for Individuals and Groups.* Kelowna: Wood Lake Publishing, 1998.

Harpur, Tom. *Prayer: The Hidden Fire.* Kelowna: Wood Lake Publishing, 1998.

Lamott, Anne. *Help, Thanks, Wow!: The Three Essential Prayers.* New York: Riverhead Books, 2012.

Meyer, Chuck. *Dying Church – Living God: A Call to Begin Again.* Kelowna: Wood Lake Publishing, 2000.

Milton, Beverley, and Margaret Kyle. *My Baptism: The Story of Jesus' Baptism and My Baptism Memories.* Kelowna: Wood Lake Publishing, 1998.

Milton, Ralph. *Angels in Red Suspenders: An Unconventional and Humorous Approach to Spirituality.* Kelowna: Wood Lake Publishing, 1997.

— *God for Beginners.* Kelowna: Wood Lake Publishing, 1996.

— *Is This Your Idea of a Good Time, God?* Kelowna: Wood Lake Publishing, 1995.

— *Man to Man: Recovering the Best of the Male Tradition.* Kelowna: Wood Lake Publishing, 1993.

— *Sermon Seasonings: Collected Stories to Spice Up Your Sermons.* Kelowna: Wood Lake Publishing, 1997.

Milton, Ralph and Margaret Kyle. *The Family Story Bible.* Kelowna: Wood Lake Publishing, 1996.

Sinclair, Donna, and Christopher White. *Jacob's Blessing: Dreams, Hopes, and Visions for the Church*. Kelowna: Wood Lake Publishing, 1999.

Taylor, James. *Everyday Parables*. Kelowna: Wood Lake Publishing, 1995.

— *Everyday Psalms: The Power of the Psalms in Language and Images for Today*. Kelowna: Wood Lake Publishing, 1993.

Your Child's Baptism. Protestant edition. Kelowna: Wood Lake Publishing.

THE AUTHOR

Dr. Ralph Milton is one of Canada's best-known religious communicators, and a recipient of an Honorary Doctorate of Sacred Letters from St. Stephen's College, Edmonton. He also has an Honorary Doctorate of Divinity from the Vancouver School of Theology. A former news broadcaster, open-line host and church administrator, Milton is the author of 17 books including the bestselling *Family Story Bible; Angels in Red Suspenders;* and *Julian's Cell,* a novel based on the life of Julian of Norwich. He recently produced a ground-breaking electronic hymnal, *Sing Hallelujah!* In retirement, Milton avidly pursues his hobby of creative photography and each week produces a series of slides to enhance the liturgy and the music at his home church, First United in Kelowna. Co-founder of Wood Lake Publishing, Ralph Milton lives in Kelowna, British Columbia, with his wife and friend of 50 years, Beverley, a retired United Church minister. Together, they remain the ever-proud grandparents of Zoë and Jake.

OTHER BOOKS BY RALPH MILTON
PUBLISHED BY WOOD LAKE
The Family Story Bible
Angels in Red Suspenders
God for Beginners
Is This Your Idea of a Good Time, God?
Julian's Cell
Man to Man
Sermon Seasonings
The Essence of Julian
Lectionary Story Bible, 3 volumes
The Spirituality of Grandparenting

WOOD LAKE

IMAGINING, LIVING, AND TELLING
THE FAITH STORY.

WOOD LAKE IS THE FAITH STORY COMPANY.

It has told
- the story of the seasons of the earth, the people of God, and the place and purpose of faith in the world;
- the story of the faith journey, from birth to death;
- the story of Jesus and the churches that carry his message.

Wood Lake has been telling stories for more than 35 years. During that time, it has given form and substance to the words, songs, pictures, and ideas of hundreds of storytellers.

Those stories have taken a multitude of forms – parables, poems, drawings, prayers, epiphanies, songs, books, paintings, hymns, curricula – all driven by a common mission of serving those on the faith journey.

Wood Lake Publishing Inc.
485 Beaver Lake Road, Kelowna, BC, Canada V4V 1S5
250.766.2778

www.woodlake.com

"A wonderful self-help book for all of us who want, and need, to know our church more deeply." – Dee Robertson, retired educator, Humboldt, SK

"As a lifetime member of the United Church, I have always appreciated the freedom to ask questions, to challenge the status quo, and to be encouraged to be creative with music and leadership. Welcome to our family of seekers and believers, and I hope that you too will feel free to ask questions on your journey. There is no 'dumb' question, because whatever you want to know has piqued your curiosity. The answer may be in this book, or you may still want to ask more when you've read it. I hope you do, and will, at a United Church near you." – Rev. Rosemary Lambie, Executive Secretary, Synode Montreal & Ottawa Conference, Montreal, Quebec

"A wonderful gift for people who are new to The United Church of Canada and for people who are active in a congregation but would like to know more about who we are." – Rev. Heather Leffler, President Elect of Hamilton Conference, Rockwood and Stone United, Rockwood, Ont.

"This book is a must-read for anyone who is curious or cares about the United Church. Ralph Milton isn't afraid to be surprised by the church he knows so well and isn't shy about acknowledging the foibles and frailties of the church he values and respects." – Rev. Elizabeth Macdonald, retired, Eastern Ontario

"A great exploration into the United Church of Canada and the diversity that can be experienced in our churches." – Barbara MacNaughton, DLM-R, Spiritual Director, Minister, St. Andrew's United Church, Easton, Sask.

"Whether you are long-time United Church or new to This United Church of Ours, *you need to read this edition. It shows us how much we have changed, how much stronger we have grown, and reminds us of the issues with which we still struggle, and why it is important to keep the faith. Ralph writes with his usual wisdom and great humour. Enjoy!"* – Rev. Lynn Maki, Executive Secretary (just retired), Alberta and Northwest Conference, Edmonton, Alta.

*"*This United Church of Ours *doesn't just tell about the United Church. It shows who we are through a writing style and stories that are personal, opinionated, humorous, and a bit risqué."* – Rev. Pegi Ridout, Interim Minister throughout Hamilton Conference, on the faculty of the Interim Ministry Network, and an associate with L3 Consulting Group

MW01046614

A PERENNIAL CA

Since its initial pubʟɪcation 35 years ago,
This United Church of Ours has been reprinted 20 times
through four editions, selling over 60,000 books.

PRAISE FOR THE FOURTH EDITION

"Ralph Milton's deep love for his church comes through on every page of this up-dated edition. Whether he's lauding the church for its many successes or criticizing it for its many shortcomings, Ralph writes with humour and honesty, all firmly grounded in a hopeful and positive future for The United Church of Canada."
– Rev. Daniel Benson, Minister, St. Paul's United Church, Scarborough, Ont.

"Milton again accepts the challenge of describing a church community which, by its evolving diversity and ever-apparent contradictions, defies description. And he succeeds by allowing us to see us as we are, through a lens of genuine affection."
– Rev. Ed Bentley, retired clergy, Belleville, Ont.

"A fun and engaging look at where the United Church of Canada is at today."
– Rt. Rev. Jordan Cantwell, Moderator, United Church of Canada

"Ralph writes of the essence of the United Church as a hopeful, humorous, irritating, stumbling, courageous, vulnerable, silly, imaginative, diverse, odd and wonderful flock of the faithful and maybe-wanna-be-faithfuls." – Rev. Jeff Cook, Minister, Transcona Memorial United Church, Winnipeg, Man.

"I have been using This United Church of Ours *to welcome and introduce people to our church for years. This 4th edition makes it possible for me to continue to use it confidently with current and updated information. It's great!"*
– Brenda Curtis DM, Westminster United Church, Humboldt, Sask.

"With wry humour and engaging writing, Ralph Milton provides an essential peek into The United Church of Canada for the newcomer as well as for those long in the pew." – Rev. Gordon Dunbar, Associate Minister for Pastoral Care and Outreach, Port Nelson United Church, Burlington, Ont. and President of Hamilton Conference